Eugene O'Neill and

Dat Ole Davil Sea

Eugene O'Neill and
Dat Ole Davil Sea

MARITIME INFLUENCES IN THE LIFE AND WORKS OF EUGENE O'NEILL

Robert A. Richter

To Sabrina
with best wishes

Robert A Richter

12/7/05

MYSTIC SEAPORT THE MUSEUM OF AMERICA AND THE SEA

Edited by Andrew W. German
Designed by Maria L. Miller

Title page:
O'Neill during his first summer in Provincetown, wearing his
crewman's sweater from the American Line, 1916 (Sheaffer-O'Neill
Collection, Connecticut College)

Mystic Seaport
75 Greenmanville Avenue
P.O. Box 6000
Mystic, CT 06355-0990

Library of Congress Cataloging-in-Publication Data

Richter, Robert A.
Eugene O'Neill and "dat ole davil sea" : maritime influences in the
life and works of Eugene O'Neill / Robert A. Richter.—1st ed.—
Mystic, CT : Mystic Seaport, c2004.
    p. : ill., ports. ; cm.
    Bibliography: p.
    Includes chronology and index.

1. O'Neill, Eugene, 1888–1953—Criticism and interpretation.
2. Dramatists, American—20th century—Biography. 3. American
drama—20th century—History and criticism. 4. Seafaring life in
literature. 5. Sailors in literature. I. Title.

    PS3529.N5 Z7935 2004

ISBN 0-939510-97-9

Contents

Preface	7
Maritime New London	11
At Home in New London	25
The Sailor's Life	
Signing On	37
Charles Racine	41
Buenos Aires	51
SS *Ikala*	58
New York	63
American Line	66
The Return to Jimmy the Priest's	74
The Return to New London	81
Maritime Provincetown	91
Arrival in Provincetown	105
Peaked Hill Bars, Bermuda, and Beyond	121
The Plays	137
Thirst, Warnings, and *Fog*	138
The Glencairn Plays	146
The Personal Equation	158
Ile	160
"Tomorrow" (short story)	164
Beyond the Horizon	166
The Rope, Where the Cross Is Made, and *Gold*	169
Chris Christophersen and *"Anna Christie"*	175
The Hairy Ape	186
Mourning Becomes Electra and "The Calms of Capricorn"	190
Conclusion	201
Notes	203
Chronology	205
Bibliography	208
Index	212

Dedication

To my father, Richard Richter,
who gave me a copy of
O'Neill's *Seven Plays of the
Sea* when I was in high
school. Neither of us knew
what a cherished book it
would become. And to my
mother, Joan Richter, who
has given me invaluable
encouragement and support.

Preface

"It was a great mistake, my being born a man,

I would have been much more successful as a sea gull or a fish."

—Edmund, *Long Day's Journey into Night*

Eugene O'Neill's maritime period spanned two years, a brief time in the life of a man who lived to be 65, but his days at sea and on shore would reverberate throughout his life and mark his work in unpredictable ways.

As America's only Nobel Prize-winning playwright and the winner of four Pulitzer Prizes, O'Neill has drawn the attention of dramatic literature scholars seeking insight into his life and into his plays, resulting in an impressive body of scholarly study and comment. O'Neill biographers, dramatic literature scholars, and theater practitioners acknowledge the importance of the maritime experience on O'Neill, but few have brought to their interpretations a comprehensive understanding of the maritime world and the culture that shaped the playwright's work. The culture of the sea has its own rules and its own vocabulary. Life at sea gives rise to a camaraderie that comes from shared experiences, under extreme pressure, unimaginable to the outsider. O'Neill's connection to the sea, and the profound effect it had on his plays, when placed in the maritime context, offers a fuller understanding of the man and his works.

It often comes as a surprise to those who do not know O'Neill's work well that 19 of his plays, out of the 45 he authorized for publication or production, are associated with the maritime world. The plays to be examined in this work are those that show a direct correlation to O'Neill's life in the maritime world. They include his early one-act plays: *Thirst, Warnings, Fog, Ile, The Rope, Where the Cross Is Made,* and the four one-act plays known as the Glencairn cycle: *Bound East for Cardiff, The Long Voyage Home, The Moon of the Caribbees,* and *In The Zone.* All the one-act plays were written between 1913 and 1918. The full-length plays explored here include *The Personal Equation* (never produced or published in O'Neill's lifetime), *Beyond the Horizon, Chris Christophersen, Gold, "Anna Christie,"*

The Hairy Ape, and *Mourning Becomes Electra* as well as the scenario for "The Calms of Capricorn." The full-length plays were written between 1915 and 1921, with the exception of *Mourning Becomes Electra,* written in 1931, and the scenario for "The Calms of Capricorn," written in 1935.

There are three plays with tangential maritime connections that will not be addressed here. They are *The Fountain* (1921), set in the late fifteen and early sixteenth centuries in Spain and Spanish America, *Marco Millions* (1925), about Marco Polo, and *Strange Interlude* (1927), where the only relationship to the maritime world is that the climactic scene takes place on the after deck of a cabin cruiser moored in the Hudson River.

This work will explore Eugene O'Neill's life and plays in the maritime context, and as a result the biographical scope is focused on a particular aspect of his life. Biographers Louis Sheaffer and Arthur and Barbara Gelb have done more extensive work on the details of his life, and this work owes a large debt to their exhaustive research. The intent here is to put O'Neill in the frame of the maritime context and to shed a sharper light on those experiences, places, and events that helped to give birth to and develop one of America's greatest playwrights; and in so doing complement the work of O'Neill scholars and clarify O'Neill's existence in the maritime world. Therefore, I have reserved the discussion of his plays for the latter half of this work. It is my intent to lay a foundation of the maritime context, which will then enable a more insightful discussion of the plays. As a point of information, ships' names appear in *italics* and the names of fictitious ships appear in *italics* with quotation marks, such as *"Glencairn."*

My work related to O'Neill began in 1988, the centennial year of his birth. Many organizations in southeastern Connecticut were collaborating to commemorate the playwright. At the time I was on staff at Mystic Seaport, and the Museum's contribution to the commemoration was staged readings of *Bound East for Cardiff* and *The Long Voyage Home,* under my direction. *Bound East for Cardiff* was performed in the fo'c's'le of the whaleship *Charles W. Morgan* and *The Long Voyage Home* was performed in the Museum's Spouter Tavern. Since we were presenting theater within the Museum I felt it important that we be able to explain to our audience the source of O'Neill's information and inspiration. O'Neill and his seafaring years came to the forefront again in 1997 when I wrote on the topic as partial fulfillment of the requirements for a Master of Arts in Liberal

Studies from Wesleyan University. Upon completion of my degree once again I moved on to other projects, but O'Neill's maritime world lingered in the background and I knew there was more to explore and say.

In 2000 the Arts Alliance of Southeastern Connecticut chose "Eugene O'Neill's New London: The Influence of Time and Place" as the theme for collaborative programming. As a result, there were eight months of lectures, performances, walking tours, and discussions revolving around O'Neill and the community of his youth. Once again my thoughts turned to O'Neill, and consequently this work emerged.

I am deeply grateful to those individuals who have encouraged and assisted in my work along the way. They include Linda Herr, professor of theater at Connecticut College, who encouraged me to stage *Bound East for Cardiff* and *The Long Voyage Home,* and the staff at Mystic Seaport who were the actors and had a deep understanding of the maritime world. Curator Sally Pavetti and Associate Curator Lois McDonald of the Eugene O'Neill Theater Center's Monte Cristo Cottage provided support, encouragement, and information, and Dr. Mary K Bercaw Edwards guided my final essay project for my degree from Wesleyan University. At the Charles E. Shain Library at Connecticut College Brian Rogers, curator emeritus, and Laurie Deredita, curator of the Sheaffer-O'Neill Collection provided their knowledge and guidance through Louis Sheaffer's research. Patricia C. Willis, curator of the Yale Collection of American Literature and the staff at Beinecke Rare Book and Manuscript Library at Yale University provided access to images and answers to many questions. William Peterson, senior curator at Mystic Seaport, Sally Ryan, New London municipal historian, and Melodie Foster, director of the New London Maritime Society shared their knowledge of New London history, and Laurel Guadazno and Jeffory Morris of Pilgrim Monument and Provincetown Museum provided guidance regarding Provincetown history and photographic images of Provincetown. Curator Cindee Herrick of the U. S. Coast Guard Museum provided access to information regarding the early years of the U. S. Life-Saving Service and Coast Guard. Paul O'Pecko and the staff of the G.W. Blunt White Library at Mystic Seaport guided me to sources on American maritime trades and ships. Andy German was a wonderful editor with valuable insight, and Richard Pickering was always available to discuss ideas and to help me develop my thoughts.

New London Lighthouse on Pequot Avenue, ca. 1890. Note the foghorn at left and the gazebo of the Pequot Casino in the background. (Mystic Seaport 1987.12.1)

Maritime New London

**"Ezra's made a pile, and before him, his father Abe Mannon,
he inherited some and made a pile more in shippin'.
Started one of the fust Western Ocean packet lines."**

—Seth Beckwith, *Mourning Becomes Electra*

During Eugene O'Neill's years in New London, the city was a maritime community in transition, shifting from primary dependence on the sea to a mixed reliance on industry and transportation. Nonetheless, 250 years after its founding, New London was steeped in its own maritime history and still looked toward the sea for economic gain. Its sea heritage was evident at every turn, from derelict ships that lay in the harbor to the steady traffic of fishing vessels, steamers, barges, yachts, and revenue cutters in the Thames River, to the palatial homes built from whaling money and the social clubs that catered to seafaring men. The families that had made, and in some cases lost, their money from the sea remained in New London and so did their stories, mundane and heroic.

In 1916, Hildegarde Hawthorne remarked that New London more closely identified "with the past era of trading and whaling and privateering and generally keeping things lively on the ocean than almost any other part of New England" (Hawthorne, 283–84). By the end of the nineteenth century, shipping had drastically decreased in New London. Yet 45 steamers, 60 schooners, 50 sloops, and 13 yachts still called the port home (Decker, 190). This is the community where the young Eugene O'Neill spent the majority of his summers. Any vessel entering or exiting New London harbor was visible from the O'Neill's front porch.

New London was founded in 1646 by John Winthrop Jr. on one of the deepest, most sheltered natural harbors on North America's Atlantic coast. The harbor was ice-free in the winter, and the Thames River provided access to the hinterland. These elements made it an ideal location for a commercial settlement. The first vessel built in New London was the *Endeavor,* which set out for the West Indies in 1661 with a cargo of local barrel staves and livestock, returning with Caribbean sugar, molasses, and rum. As Connecticut's leading port, New London maintained a flourishing trade with the West Indies until the Revolutionary War, when the British Royal Navy blockaded New London harbor.

During the Revolution, New London ship owners turned to privateering, licensed to prey on British merchant ships. Captured, the ship and its contents became the property of the privateer, and the seized ship and cargo were sold in town, enriching the entire community. But privateering led to the burning of New London toward the end of the war, in September of 1781. After New Londoners captured the ship *Hanna,* loaded with goods that included personal items destined for British officers in New York, the former American hero and now British commander Benedict Arnold led a raid on New London. Arnold was familiar with the territory, having been born in Norwich, just up the Thames from New London. Arnold's forces burned most of the warehouses, wharves, and vessels on the waterfront and massacred the militia stationed at Fort Griswold on the Groton side of the river. By the end of the day, New London was almost completely destroyed.

After the Treaty of Paris concluded the Revolutionary War in 1783, New London tried to revive the West Indies trade in farm produce and livestock for sugar and rum, though American ships were excluded from the British islands. By the end of the War of 1812—the second American Revolution—New London was out of the West Indies trade. So in 1819 New London merchants revived another prewar maritime industry—whaling. New London whalemen were particularly known for their fearless pursuit into the distant regions of the ocean—the North Pacific, the South Indian Ocean, and Davis Strait and Hudson Bay in the eastern Arctic. By the 1840s New London became one of the largest whaling ports in the United States, second only to New Bedford, Massachusetts. Several families, including the Allyns, the Williamses, and the Lawrences, derived fortunes from whaling that contributed to the port's cultural and social organization. As in the nation as a whole, New London's whaling industry reached its peak in 1846, but it continued until the schooner *Margarett* completed her last New London voyage in 1909.

When the *Margarett* set out on her last New London voyage O'Neill was 21 and on the verge of going to sea himself. He had had the opportu-

**Captain James W. Buddington and the crew of the whaling schooner
Margarett, September 1908 (Mystic Seaport 1939.1305.2)**

nity to observe the end of New London whaling and absorb some of its
lore. Hildegarde Hawthorne, writing about the heyday of New London
whaling, said:

> Every returning ship was greeted with frantic scenes of joy.
> As soon as her bow rounded the headlands of Fisher's Island
> her signal flags told who she was, and the town streamed
> down to her wharf. Sometimes a heavy tale was brought for
> the hearing, for the long hard voyages, enduring for years,
> had much tragedy and loss. But at least some had come safe
> to home and wife, and their share of the gold-bringing oil in
> the hold (Hawthorne, 276).

It was not only the crew's families that joined in on the excitement of a
returning ship. The ownership of a whaler was divided into 36 shares, and
many members of the community invested. The crew was also invested
in their ship. They were paid on a lay system and received a share of the
profits at the completion of a voyage. The lays ranged from 1/8 of the pro-
ceeds for the captain to 1/150 for a foremast hand (Decker, 87). In most

instances the captain also had a share in the ownership of the vessel. The financial gain of the crew was based on their skill and luck. If the ship had been unlucky it was not uncommon for a foremast hand, who received an advance on his earnings at the outset of the voyage, to come back indebted to the ship.

Merchants and skilled craftsmen played a significant role in outfitting a ship for a voyage and might take a share of the profits for payment, provide goods on credit, or be paid outright. Boardinghouse keepers and outfitters received the sailors' advance pay to settle accounts and to provide a basic—and often shoddy—outfit of seagoing clothes and foul weather gear. Upon the sailors' return the hotels, boardinghouses, and bars along the waterfront prospered as the seamen took over the town. With the success of a whaling expedition the whole community flourished.

New England whalemen did not venture out of the Atlantic Ocean until the end of the 1700s. As whales became scarce and the demand for whale products increased, they began sailing around the Cape of Good Hope into the Indian Ocean, venturing around Cape Horn into the Pacific Ocean, reaching Japan and Hawai'i about 1820, and following whales into the Arctic Ocean after 1848. New London whalemen became specialists at hunting whales in Davis Strait and Hudson Bay in the eastern Arctic, and in hunting elephant seals at Kerguelen and Heard Islands in the far southern Indian Ocean. When the American whaling industry reached its peak in 1846, there were 736 whalers operating. The greater New Bedford, Massachusetts, area accounted for more than 400 of those vessels, while New London was second with 70 ships (Albion, 116). Throughout its whaling years, from the 1790s to 1909, New London had approximately 260 whaling ships (Decker, 87).

Great wealth could be made through whaling. Captain Ebenezer "Rattler" Morgan had a career that spanned 41 years. He began in 1827, at the age of 10, and by the time he was 21 he had become a captain. He received the nickname "Rattler" for rapid speech and "rattling" good voyages. He made the most lucrative whaling voyage on record from 1864 to 1865. The investment for the voyage was $35,800, and at the end of the 15-month voyage the cargo sold for $150,000. Towards the end of his career in 1866 he commanded the first American steam whaler, the *Pioneer*. At his death in 1890 his estate was valued at nearly $1,000,000 (Decker, 82).

One of the wealthiest merchants in the state of Connecticut was New London whaling agent Sebastian Lawrence, whose father had arrived as an immigrant Italian grocer and began the whaling investments that his sons continued so successfully. At the time of his death in 1909, Sebastian Lawrence's estate was valued at $10,000,000. Some of his money went to organizations in town, including $50,000 for an almshouse, $15,000 to St. James Church, $1,000 to the New London County Historical Society, and $1,000 to the Jibboom Club, a maritime fraternal organization (Decker, 160).

A diverse mix of men of many different nationalities, ethnicities, social backgrounds, and education levels could be found in any whaling crew. Especially in its early years of growth, some men went whaling as a way to advance through the ranks and amass a sizable income. John Rice, known as "Boney" because he had a great admiration for Napoleon Bonaparte, began his whaling career in 1819 at the age of 21 as a greenhand, or inexperienced sailor, and on his fourth voyage, at the age of 24, he sailed as captain. Over his 40-year whaling career he sailed for all the major New London companies (Decker, 82).

Others looked to whaling as a way to straighten out a wayward son. In an 1857 letter, John Ross wrote to Sebastian Lawrence, "I am sorry to inform you that my son is giving me a good deal of unnecessary trouble by his bad habits, so much so that I am determined to send him on a long voyage to sea in a whaling vessel or something of the kind" (Decker, 86).

As whalemen had to travel farther to find whales, whaling voyages increased in length from perhaps 18 months to 36 or even 48 months or more. Married crew members and their families had to endure longer separations, and whaling wives learned a degree of independence in the effort to support themselves. Whaling ports like New London often had a proportion of women living alone and operating businesses, from teaching to shopkeeping. An increasing number of captains brought their wives to sea with them. Rattler Morgan and Boney Rice both sailed with their wives at least once. When Nancy Bolles accompanied her husband in 1850–53, she left with two children and returned with two more who had been born in Hawai'i. As the crossroads for Pacific whalemen, the Hawai'ian Islands—as well as other Pacific ports—figured prominently in New London maritime history. Several local men migrated to the islands to set up whaling related businesses. Ships transported supplies and crew from New London to the Pacific and returned with whale products that had been off-loaded in the Hawai'ian Islands for transshipment. The link with the Pacific lasted until 1922 when the Atlantic and Western Steamship Company discontinued service from New London (Decker, 208).

Additional businesses in New London that supported whaling included boatshops and a biscuit company. The highly regarded Rogers Boat Shop on Bank Street supplied whaleboats for whaleships from 1832 until 1894. Rogers retired at the age of 79 when the need for whaleboats had declined. But there was enough demand for Captain William H. Burdick to open a shop on Howard Street in 1896, which remained in business until 1902 (Decker, 168–70).

Beginning in 1831 the C.D. Boss Company, located on Water Street, produced biscuits and crackers, and during the whaling years their major business was supplying ship's biscuit, or hardtack, the principal form of bread carried on board ships. A fire destroyed the bakery in 1864, but within three months Boss was back in business in one of the most modern bakeries in the country. The company diversified its offerings over the years to produce everything from lemon cake to a patented lunch milk biscuit called the Boston Soda Cracker. Baked in New London, Boss crackers were distributed nationally until 1911, when labor problems and stiff competition from the National Biscuit Company caused the Boss firm to dissolve and sell the rights to its products to their competitor, now known as Nabisco (Decker, 114).

New London's principal maritime industry, whaling, declined for several reasons. The success of the industry was partially to blame. As whale populations were killed off, whalemen had to travel farther and longer to fill their ships. Longer and less profitable voyages meant that crews became more marginalized, with fewer opportunities to advance. To find crews, shipping agents reached out to rural farming communities to entice men with the opportunity to see the world on a whaling ship. In many instances, New England whaleships filled out their crews in the Azores or Cape Verde Islands. Ships whaling in the Pacific recruited Hawai'ians or other islanders, referred to generally as Kanakas ("people" in Hawai'ian), to replace deserters or otherwise complete their crews.

Beyond labor problems, the most aggressive whaling merchants found it more lucrative to reinvest their whaling profits in railroad construction, in textile mills, in insurance, or in the other developing industries. Without significant reinvestment, the industry began to contract.

For the first half of the 1800s, sperm oil was the most valuable whaling product. Compressed into bright, clean-burning candles or refined into lamp oil or lubricating oil, it had an important place in the home, in factories, and even in lighthouses that assisted navigation. But after the extraction and refining of petroleum were perfected in 1859, petroleum products such as kerosene and lubricating oil began to undercut whale oil's place in the market. However, the long strips of baleen found in the mouths of the right whales commonly taken by New London whalemen became increasingly valuable as oil declined. Processed into a wide variety of flexible products, from buggy whips to corset stays, this "whalebone" sustained the industry until spring steel was developed for similar uses shortly after 1900.

The Civil War took its toll on the whaling fleet. The federal government purchased 45 surplus whaling vessels, 11 of which were from New London; had them filled with stone; and ordered them sunk to blockade the Southern ports of Charleston and Savannah. This unsuccessful effort reduced the fleet of whaleships, as did Confederate commerce raiders, which sank five New London whaleships.

The weather also took its toll on whaling. In 1871, 39 ships, including four New London vessels, were trapped in an early freeze by ice while whaling in the Arctic Ocean. When the ice began to crush the ships the crews abandoned them and escaped in whaleboats. The ships and their cargoes were a total loss amounting to $2,000,000 (Decker, 91).

With a reduced fleet, reduced involvement, and reduced demand for its products, the whaling industry was a marginal one by 1900. New London continued to send out a vessel or two until 1909, when the schooner *Margarett* set out.

During the period Eugene O'Neill frequented New London, the city was a maritime community in transition. There was much of interest for him to observe and think about. Whaling had declined, but a variety of maritime endeavors prevailed, including fishing, shipbuilding, military, yachting, and the distribution of goods. The city's fishing fleet was significant, including between 40 and 50 vessels. They fished primarily in local waters for halibut, cod, and swordfish. Occasionally they sailed to Georges Bank to fish in the North Atlantic. New London was a distribution point. Boats from other communities came to unload and sell their catch or have it transshipped to other markets, such as New York.

The New London Board of Trade lobbied long and hard to have the U.S. Navy establish a base in New London. In 1872, the navy erected two buildings and a pier on the Groton side of the Thames and established a navy yard, which developed into a coaling station for naval vessels by the 1890s. The first United States Marine Corps training school was established at the navy yard in 1900, remaining there until 1915. In 1916 the navy designated the site the nation's first continental submarine base.

The United States Revenue Cutter Service established its training facility at Fort Trumbull in New London. The Revenue Cutter Service and the U.S. Life-Saving Service merged in 1915 to become the U.S. Coast Guard. The training facility at Fort Trumbull became the Coast Guard Academy, where it remained until moving to its current location in another part of New London in 1931.

Shipbuilding, always a part of the activity in New London, saw a small revival in the 1890s. In April of 1900 the Eastern Shipbuilding Company leased land across the river in Groton with the intent of building large ships. The company had a contract to build two 622-foot steel steamships for $5,000,000. The *Minnesota* was launched in April 1903 and the *Dakota* in February 1904. Designed for transpacific service, they were the largest cargo vessels in the world at the time, and the launchings attracted large crowds and attention. The New London Ship and Engine Company took over the site in 1910 and by 1911 employed 300 men making heavy oil engines. This was the first company in the United States to produce marine diesel engines (Decker, 171).

With the increasing industrialization of the Northeast, coal became the principal coastwise shipping commodity. Coal-fired boilers powered industrial machinery, coal-fired power plants produced electricity, and coal-fired furnaces warmed urban homes and commercial buildings. Though it was still shipped north from Philadelphia and Chesapeake Bay in large coasting schooners under sail, by the 1890s an increasing amount of coal was carried in barges towed by large tugboats.

The Thames Tow Boat Company was a significant enterprise for New London, handling most of the coal coming into New London and nearby ports. As an indication of the volume of the coal that traveled by barge, at the turn of the twentieth century the Robert Palmer and Son shipyard of Noank, just east of New London, launched 140 schooner barges between 1890 and 1915. Some of them were built for the Thames Tow Boat Company (Morris, 23). In 1903 the Thames Tow Boat Company launched the tug *Paul Jones* in New London. Built at the peak of wooden tug construction, the *Paul Jones* measured 192 feet in length, drew 18 feet, and had a steam engine that could develop 1,600 horsepower, giving her a speed of 16 knots. Smaller tugs could handle one or two barges. Large

Employees of the Thames Tow Boat Company, ca. 1900 (Mystic Seaport 1984.4.4)

oceangoing towboats like the *Paul Jones* could pull four to six barges in moderate summer weather and two to four in winter.

Schooner barges had the efficient shape of a sailing vessel and were rigged with small fore-and-aft sails, but they were not intended to sail themselves. When the wind was favorable the sails aided in the towing, and in the event a schooner barge was separated from the tow, which was not uncommon, they had some maneuverability. To handle a schooner barge, which might measure between 150 and 300 feet in length, a crew of four to seven lived in a house aft, steered, stood watch, and attended to the sails and to the towlines that linked it to the towboat or the other barges in the string.

Depending on the weather and the length of the tow, the tug might not be able to see the barges toward the end of the tow and would be

Barges and coasting schooners are anchored in the Thames River off New

unaware if the towline parted. Long tows could be a menace to other shipping, resulting in collisions, particularly at night or in fog. The Thames Tow Boat Company tug *Argo* brought a long tow of barges from Norfolk, Virginia, and when it arrived in New London it was discovered that one of the barges was missing. After anchoring the remaining barges, the *Argo* went back out in search of the missing one. Near Montauk Point, Long Island, the schooner barge was sighted slowly making its way to New London under sail (Morris, 71).

Barges, and the lives of people that worked on them play a significant role in O'Neill's *Chris Christophersen* and *"Anna Christie."*

In addition to maritime-related businesses, New London had social organizations that catered to seafaring men, in particular the Jibboom

London in this view from Fort Griswold, ca. 1905 (Mystic Seaport 1977.92.39)

Club. Begun in 1871 as a fraternal organization dedicated to providing an opportunity for social engagement among its members—officers from whaling vessels—it was formally organized on 29 January 1891, with 111 members. By 1901 membership exceeded 300. At its inception the criterion for membership was at least two years of experience at sea. New members were initiated into the club with a ceremony based on the crossing-the-line ceremony that was common aboard merchant ships. Sailors crossing the equator for the first time were brought before "King Neptune" and received into his court. Neptune and members of his court were played by disguised and costumed members of the crew. In many cases the initiate would be blindfolded, his face would be "lathered" with tar and "shaved," and then he would be pushed into a large tub of seawater before being presented to the king. With the decline in New London's maritime trades, the two-year sea experience requirement for Jibboom Club membership was dropped in 1913. The club convened bimonthly, presided over by the commodore or captain, while the steward was responsible for making coffee, chowder, and plum duff—a boiled or steamed pudding made with flour, which when served aboard ship was considered a treat, and with the addition of raisins for sweetness became plum duff (Oliver, 109). Between meetings, club members gathered at the club-rooms in downtown New London to play board games and cards, tell stories, and sing chanteys. The club did not allow any members to drink alcohol or play cards for money in the club-rooms.

The club did encourage singing, especially of chanteys. For a number of years someone held the unofficial title of club chantey master. At sea, chanteys were sung only to spur the work effort, but for the retired sailors they were nostalgic reminders of the age of sail. The club members' favorite chantey was "Santa Anna," which was sung regularly at meetings.

The club held an annual parade in honor of George Washington's birthday. A band, floats, and members in costume marched along Bank Street and up State Street, two of the main arteries in downtown New London. The club membership dwindled after World War I, and the organization finally disbanded in 1959, but its longevity was a testament to New Londoners' pride and interest in the city's maritime heritage.

O'Neill would have known some of the Jibboomers and witnessed their festivities. It is easy to imagine him absorbing details, which he stored

The Jibboom Club parade, ca. 1910 (Mystic Seaport 1986.94.325)

away for later use in his writing. Whether or not he heard the Jibboom Club members sing, O'Neill would use a variety of chanteys in a number of his plays.

There were other maritime notables in the New London community that O'Neill would have known or been aware of. One of those was his father's friend Captain Nat Keeney, an old seaman who owned a fish market. He was known for his rough language and stories. A member of a whaling family, Keeney might have served for part of the inspiration, if only in name, for Captain Keeney, the hard-driving whaling captain in O'Neill's *Ile*.

**Young Eugene O'Neill overlooking the Thames River in New London, ca. 1896
(Sheaffer–O'Neill Collection, Connecticut College)**

At Home In New London

". . . this town's not so bad. I like it well enough.
I suppose because it's the only home we've had."

—Edmund, *Long Day's Journey into Night*

James O'Neill was a rising star of the American theater when he and his wife Ella purchased two New London properties in 1884, four years before their youngest son Eugene was born. James's career was going well; so too was his life with Ella. The year before, the 37-year-old actor had stepped into the leading role of Edmund Dantes in *The Count of Monte Cristo,* replacing an ailing Charles Thorne, the production's scheduled star. While theater critics found little of interest in the play, audiences loved the melodrama, and tremendous box-office profits kept James O'Neill touring in the play for more than 20 years. The role of Edmund Dantes may have brought fame and fortune, but the role stunted James O'Neill's growth as a Shakespearean actor, something he deeply regretted. In *Long Day's Journey into Night,* set in New London in 1912, his son Eugene would give voice to that regret when James Tyrone confesses to his son Edmund, "my good bad luck made me find the big money-maker" (O'Neill, CP3, 810).

James O'Neill invested well in real estate. In New London, land values increased between 50 and 200 percent between 1885 and 1888. Located halfway between New York and Boston, New London had become an attractive town with a sewer system, modern hotels, paved streets, and regular steamboat and railroad connections to New York City (Decker, 131). The city was growing as a resort community, and some summer visitors settled as permanent residents.

James and Ella O'Neill already had friends and family in New London when the actor bought the property on Pequot Avenue. Ella's mother had recently moved there to be near her sister, and James's old friend John McGinley was working as a reporter for the *New London Day.* Comfortable in the community, James contracted with local carpenters

Ella Quinlan O'Neill (Sheaffer–O'Neill
Collection, Connecticut College)

James O'Neill as the Count of Monte
Cristo, ca. 1900 (Sheaffer–O'Neill
Collection, Connecticut College)

and plumbers to make improvements to the kitchen and parlor of their
home, and install indoor plumbing before he left on the 1885 western
tour of *Monte Cristo*.

In 1900 the O'Neills moved into their other, larger house, just two
doors down the street. It was a property James already owned and had
been renting. Both homes were located on the fringe of the more exclusive Pequot Colony, a summer resort. The resort colony had grown up
around the Pequot House, a summer hotel that opened in 1853. Overlooking Fishers Island Sound and the mouth of the Thames River, and
cooled by ocean breezes, the hotel attracted wealthy New Yorkers and
drew an elite clientele from as far away as Washington, D.C. The Pequot
House became so popular that it built cottages for extended rentals.
Eventually, the Pequot House and its surrounding cottages could host 600
people. Then, as more and more private cottages were constructed nearby, the area became known as the Pequot Colony.

As a focus for their social activities, the prominent families who
owned summer cottages in the Pequot Colony established the Pequot
Casino Association in 1890. They acquired waterfront property and built

a spacious "casino"–clubhouse–with courts for the newly popular game of tennis, a billiard room, a ballroom, and two dining rooms. At the water's edge, a long pier ran out to a large gazebo built on a rock ledge in the Thames River. The moonlit Pequot Casino pier serves as the setting for the Prologue and Epilogue of O'Neill's play *The Great God Brown*. The Pequot Casino represented a social world where an Irish touring actor, like James O'Neill and his family, would never be welcomed, no matter his fame, and the playwright's sense of exclusion is clearly expressed in the play's Epilogue when he describes his characters as listening to "the sound of the waves" and the Casino's "distant dance music" (O'Neill, CP2, 534).

In their own home, dubbed the Monte Cristo Cottage by James, the family gathered strength between exhausting theatrical tours. Always on the move, Eugene and his older brother, Jamie, were either on tour with their parents or in boarding schools. But in the summer they had the comfort of waking up in the same room each day, which overlooked

Pequot House and bathhouses, New London, ca. 1880 (Mystic Seaport 1984.10.2)

Pequot Avenue with the Casino and its pier and gazebo in the foreground and New London Lighthouse in the background, ca. 1900 (Mystic Seaport 1976.166.398)

the water and lay between the social elite of the rustic Pequot Colony to the south and the bustling city streets of New London to the north.

There was tragedy beneath the surface of the family. Shortly after Eugene was born, Ella became addicted to morphine, which had been prescribed by the hotel doctor attending her at his birth. She struggled with the addiction for many years. According to O'Neill biographer Stephen Black, Ella had greater difficulty with her addiction in the latter half of the 1890s, and being near her New London relatives exacerbated the problem. To relieve the strain, the O'Neills rented cottages in the

Catskills, on Staten Island, or at the New Jersey shore on several occasions, but for the most part they returned to New London for the summer.

A strong presence stood just south of the Pequot Colony in the form of New London Lighthouse. First built in 1790, the brick tower guided shipping to the mouth of the Thames River. Nightly, the light flashed out, and during the region's frequent summer fogs the light's steam-powered foghorn blared out. Even when the foghorn was moved in 1909 to the new Ledge Light—built atop a wave-swept ledge on the east side of the shipping channel—summer residents complained about the foghorn's noise. The foghorn could be heard at the O'Neill home, and it appears to torment Mary Tyrone in *Long Day's Journey into Night*. "It's the foghorn I hate. It won't let you alone," she tells Cathleen, the maid. "It keeps reminding you, and warning you, and calling you back. But it can't tonight. It's just an ugly sound. It doesn't remind me of anything" (O'Neill, CP3, 773). About a year before O'Neill started to work on *Long Day's Journey into Night* in 1939, he commented about foghorns during an interview. "I like them. They keep some people awake but they put me to sleep" (Sheaffer, SA, 458).

Eugene, Jamie, and James O'Neill on the porch of the Monte Cristo Cottage, ca. 1900 (Sheaffer-O'Neill Collection, Connecticut College)

O'Neill accompanied his parents on his father's theatrical tours until the age of seven. He then attended St. Aloysius, a boys' boarding school located on the campus of Mount St. Vincent, a larger school for girls just north of Manhattan in the Riverdale section of the Bronx, overlooking the Hudson River. According to Sheaffer, Sister Mary Florentine, O'Neill's teacher, recalled him as being quiet, reserved, and polite. He generally kept to himself, reading or watching the boat traffic on the river. But he came to life when she took them to the Hudson for a swim (Sheaffer, SP, 65). At the school his favorite books were Rudyard Kipling's *The Jungle Books* (published in 1894 and 1895) and *Captains Courageous* (published in 1897). His attraction to *Captains Courageous* (the story of a wealthy boy who falls overboard from a luxury liner in a fog and learns about life and responsibility on board a Gloucester fishing schooner) is particularly telling given his own seafaring experiences and writings later in life.

At age 12, O'Neill entered De La Salle Academy in New York City as a day student and lived with his parents in a residential hotel. Two years later, he transferred to Betts Academy in Stamford, Connecticut, which limited its enrollment to 60 pupils and provided a one-to-five teacher-student ratio. O'Neill enjoyed Betts. Its philosophy was to inspire "each [student] to proceed as his own rate, and to cultivate in them sound habits of observation and research." In observation, the school's brochure stated: "the first task of the student is the inspection of things that are constantly before him, such as plants, animals, the stars, etc. He is thus taught first to see and then to tell what he sees going on around him in nature and the practical life, and is required to record his observation in well-systematized books" (Gelbs, LWMC, 170).

During his summers in New London, Eugene O'Neill was engaged in a number of activities, both with the summer elite and with the downtown locals. In August 1905, Eugene wrote to Marion Welch, a young woman from Hartford whom he had met while she was visiting one of the O'Neills' neighbors: "I was up to one of the 'hops' at the Pequot last Saturday night and danced with the fair ones (not even fair). I was bored to death and said 'Never again for little Eugene' and by the nine gods I never will unless you or someone else that I know are there."[1]

After his graduation from Betts, 17-year-old O'Neill stayed in New London for the summer with his brother Jamie while their parents were in England. Black says that "Jamie spent his summer drinking and whoring, and Eugene followed suit" (Black, 88). Jamie was ten years Eugene's senior and certainly capable of introducing his brother to the seamier side of New London as Stephen Black suggests he did.

The center of New London's underworld was Bradley Street, near the city's commercial street, State Street, not far from the railroad station and steamboat docks. At the turn of the twentieth century, traveling salesmen reported that New London had "the liveliest, most wide-open red light district" on the route from New York to Boston (Sheaffer, SP, 59). Bradley Street was the district's hub; ironically the police headquarters was also located there. Addie Burns's place on Bradley Street was a particular favorite of the O'Neill boys, and Addie herself was immortalized in *Long Day's Journey into Night* as Mamie Burns. O'Neill was perhaps rehearsing a scene from his adolescence when he had Jamie Tyrone describe his visit to Mamie Burns's place:

> Guess which one of Mamie's charmers I picked to bless me with her woman's love. It'll hand you a laugh kid. I picked Fat Violet . . . soon as I got in the door, Mamie began telling me all her troubles. Beefed how rotten business was, and she was going to give Fat Violet the gate. Customers didn't fall for Vi. One reason she'd kept her was she could play the piano. . . . Well, that made me feel sorry for Fat Violet, so I squandered two bucks of your dough to escort her upstairs. (O'Neill, CP3, 816).

In O'Neill's youth a New London prostitute named Violet played piano in one of the Bradley Street establishments.

O'Neill's time in New London was not spent solely in bars and brothels. Unlike his brother Jamie, he enjoyed the water, both swimming and rowing. Margaret Kiley, who lived nearby, recalled O'Neill as a "fish, a regular water rat, forever playing around in the water" (Sheaffer, SP, 59). The Monte Cristo Cottage gave O'Neill easy access to the water. Beyond the exclusive Pequot Colony was Ocean Beach, another growing resort community. The trolley line was extended from downtown New London to Ocean Beach in 1892, which made it more accessible and popular. O'Neill and his friends spent many happy days along the boardwalk, dancing by the bandstand, or watching fireworks displays during festivals.

Ocean Beach, New London, ca. 1910 (Mystic Seaport 1994.1.3)

One of the annual early-summer events in New London was the Harvard-Yale boat race, held on the Thames River in June. The crews raced in eight-oared shells over a four-mile course north of the new railroad bridge across the river. The day of the rowing race—"boat day"—brought out a large crowd of celebrants and spectators, as described by Hildegarde Hawthorne.

> The river crowded up to the edges of the course, with yachts of every caliber, each decorated with every shred of bunting in the owner's possession. Rowboats loaded to the gunwales, canoes rocking on the slight swell of the tide, the Judge's launch bustling importantly back and forth. A ship or two belonging to the Navy looking on in calm dignity. . . . Each year the crowds gather, turning New London into a cross between a country fair and a college commencement, the rival shells flash down or up the course, crimson or blue triumphs, and all, even the losers have a perfectly gorgeous time. For a whole day the old town plays like a child in the sun, youth fills its streets and camps on its verandas, while even the oldest inhabitant acts as though the most important thing in the world was just that possible inch or two between

the leading and the beaten boat. Nothing of this sort is known to any other town in New England (Hawthorne, 265–67).

If they were in New London, the O'Neills most likely were wrapped up in the day's events just as everyone else was. Certainly O'Neill recalled the day in his writings, using "boat day" as the backdrop for the climactic scene in *Strange Interlude.*

In the fall of 1906, O'Neill entered Princeton University. His university career was brief, spent more in socializing than in studying.

The Harvard-Yale boat race on the Thames River, ca. 1905 (Mystic Seaport 1979.35)

Stephen Black mentions that O'Neill decorated his room at Princeton by draping a piece of fishnet on the wall and hanging on it actresses' slippers, tights, bras, stockings, and "scandalous posters and publicity posters of noted chanteuses" (Black, 91). There is no doubt that O'Neill would have felt comfortable socializing with actresses in New York. He had known actresses on his father's tours, and because he was the son of the famous actor they welcomed his company.

While at Princeton, O'Neill explored the bars in Greenwich Village and Hell's Kitchen in New York City, and struck up an acquaintance with Louis Holladay. Holladay lived with his older sister Polly, who owned and operated various restaurants in Greenwich Village. O'Neill often stayed with the Holladays in New York on weekends. It was through the Holladays that O'Neill would eventually make his entrée into the bohemian set in the Village and later Provincetown.

Eugene O'Neill was suspended from Princeton in the spring of 1907 for "poor scholastic standing" after he failed to take his final exams. He returned to New London and did not go back to college. But, O'Neill never stopped educating himself. In New London, O'Neill read the poems of Ernest Dowson, Edward FitzGerald, Algernon Swinburne, Charles Baudelaire, and Oscar Wilde and also read the literature and political theory of George Bernard Shaw, Karl Marx, Friedrich Engels, Fyodor Dostoyevsky, Leo Tolstoy, Maksim Gorky, Joseph Conrad, and Jack London. Stephen Black suggests that reading Conrad and London probably led O'Neill to the works of Herman Melville years before Melville would be rediscovered by scholars (Black, 87).

In 1907, there were few places in New London where one could find such a range of modern literature and political theory. O'Neill was probably introduced to these authors by the Second Story Club, a group of friends who gathered in Dr. Joe Ganey's second-story apartment above his office on Main Street. Ed Keefe, "Ice" Casey, "Hutch" Collins, Scott Linsley, and Art and Tom McGinley were members of the club. Many remained O'Neill's lifelong friends. O'Neill's only comedy, *Ah, Wilderness!*, was partially based on the McGinley family.

Members of the Second Story Club played cards, drank, and read from "Doc" Ganey's personal library. During his travels abroad, Ganey had acquired first editions, many of them avant garde works banned in

Members of the Second Story Club (from left) Andy Spellman, Hutch Collins, Frank Mix, Doc Ganey, Ed Keefe, D. Belcher, Tom McGinley, Scott Linsley, ca. 1912 (Sheaffer–O'Neill Collection, Connecticut College)

the United States. O'Neill read extensively in the doctor's library, though Ganey resisted the young man's desire to borrow rare books. The Second Story Club was seen as New London's bohemian center. In the summer the group might meet at Ganey's cottage on the Niantic River in nearby East Lyme. Ganey flouted convention by living openly with his mistress, Kate, who recalled of O'Neill: "Gene . . . sitting on the railing and looking at the river, the boats going by, as if he was miles away—that was typical of him" (Sheaffer, SP, 225).

During this time, Second Story Club member and artist Ed Keefe introduced O'Neill to George Bellows, the painter who later became the leader of the Ashcan School. Keefe and Bellows shared an apartment in New York while they were both art students, and O'Neill stayed with them on occasion. In January 1909 the three young men moved out to Zion, New Jersey, to live in a rundown farmhouse owned by James O'Neill. They hoped that the seclusion of the rural setting would give the two artists an opportunity to paint and O'Neill time to write. The living accommodations turned out to be too rustic, however, and the three returned to New York after about a month.

The ship *Timandra* departs Boston with a load of lumber for Buenos Aires. While O'Neill was in Buenos Aires in 1910 he worked briefly loading the ship with hides. With her bucko mate, white hull, and main skysail (furled at the top of the mast in this photograph), she is the likely inspiration for the *"Amindra"* in *The Long Voyage Home*. (Peabody Essex Museum)

The Sailor's Life

"We'd be making sail in the dawn, with a fair breeze,
singing a chanty song wid no care to it.
And astern the land would be sinking and dying out,
but we'd give it no heed but a laugh, and never a look behind."

—Paddy, *The Hairy Ape*

SIGNING ON

When he was in Greenwich Village in the spring of 1909, friends introduced O'Neill to a young woman named Kathleen Jenkins. Age 20 like
O'Neill, Kathleen was from a respectable family, but her parents were
estranged and she lived with her mother. She found O'Neill "different"
and "very romantic," and they spent a great deal of time together, taking
long walks along Riverside Drive in Manhattan (Sheaffer, SP, 144). When
Kathleen learned that she was pregnant in September of that year, O'Neill
offered to marry her. He was young, unemployed, and had no idea of
what career he might pursue, and no doubt he was aware that his father
would not approve of the marriage. So the couple agreed to keep it secret
and was married in Hoboken, New Jersey, on 2 October 1909. A few days
after the wedding, O'Neill left for Honduras on a prospecting trip that
was financed by his father (Black, 100–102). While O'Neill was in
Honduras he learned through letters from his father and Kathleen that
the two families had found out about the marriage and knew that she was
expecting a child (Sheaffer, SP, 155–56).

Distance cooled his desire. When he returned from Honduras in
the spring, O'Neill made no effort to contact his wife. According to Louis
Kalonyme, who interviewed the playwright in 1924, O'Neill went to one
of the bars he frequented in New York and, on seeing O'Neill, the bartender announced that drinks were on the house. O'Neill asked the
bartender the reason for his generosity. The bartender handed him a copy
of *The World* newspaper, which had the story of Eugene Jr.'s birth, and

stated that the father was in Honduras prospecting for gold (Gelb, LWMC, 272). When the Jenkins family realized that O'Neill was back in New York and had not been in touch with Kathleen, they blamed James O'Neill for keeping his son away from his wife and child. They knew that James was opposed to the marriage, believing that Kathleen and her mother were after his money. When James appointed Eugene assistant company manager for the production of *The White Sister,* which soon took him on tour, he strengthened their belief that he was trying to keep his son away from his new family (Gelb, 139–40).

While Eugene was in Boston with *The White Sister,* the press took up the story of his marriage to Kathleen and the birth of a son he had never seen. The coverage that followed resulted in negative publicity for both Eugene and James O'Neill, but because of his celebrity as an actor the bad press was more detrimental to the elder O'Neill.

During *The White Sister*'s run in Boston, O'Neill met sailors from the *Charles Racine* and learned that the *Racine* occasionally carried unofficial passengers. Eugene persuaded his father that it would be a good experience for him to go to sea (Sheaffer, SP, 160). The idea struck James O'Neill as a way of ending the run of bad publicity—a motive similar to that of

The Norwegian bark *Charles Racine,* on which O'Neill sailed from Boston to Buenos Aires in 1910 (Sheaffer-O'Neill Collection, Connecticut College)

earlier New London families who sent troublesome sons on a whaling voyage, hoping it would straighten them out. So it was almost by happenstance that Eugene boarded the *Charles Racine* to begin his time at sea.

It is appropriate to use the phrase "time at sea" because O'Neill's role on board ship is unclear. Was he actually employed as a sailor? In some respects the answer is immaterial. There is no doubt that his experiences and knowledge were that of a sailor or that he earned the rank of Able Bodied Seaman, an achievement of which he was deeply proud. A close look at the details of his experiences as a sailor, at sea and ashore, will better frame O'Neill in the maritime context and illuminate its tremendous impact on his life and literary works.

Aboard merchant sailing vessels, sailors who were not officers were ranked as Boy, Ordinary Seaman, or Able Bodied Seaman (Shay, 104). A Boy was the most inexperienced of the deckhands. Though title did not denote age, in many cases those in this position were the youngest on board. An Ordinary Seaman had learned some of the duties of the trade but had not acquired the specific skills of an Able Bodied Seaman. A sailor might be eligible for the rank of Ordinary Seaman after his first voyage or after having served some time as a Boy, usually a year or two (Weibust, 296). An Able Bodied Seaman was the most skilled of all the deckhands. Both an Ordinary and an Able Bodied Seaman were expected to have an understanding of all the standing and running rigging and to be able to furl and reef sails, steer, "box the compass"—recite the 32 directional coordinates on the compass—and rig gear for, and set, particular sails. One distinction between the Ordinary and Able Bodied Seaman was that the junior man was only required to furl and reef sails single-handedly and to steer under common conditions. In severe weather conditions the more experienced Able Bodied Seaman would handle those functions (Shay, 108).

No firm rules governed promotions aboard sailing ships. In the merchant service each ship had a specified number of positions for each rating. The individual who wanted the position signed on by putting his name down for the position and contracting for the wages and duties of one of the three rates. There was little checking of qualifications, but also little abuse of the system. If someone signed on for a position for which he was not qualified, his inexperience would soon become obvious to the entire crew and officers. He would be demoted and fined, and might suffer the wrath of the other sailors, who would have to work harder because of the dishonesty of a colleague (Shay, 104). This was the world in which O'Neill would soon find himself.

There were many ships to choose from in Boston Harbor, but the *Charles Racine* stood out. Since the 1880s, steamships had taken over the world's transoceanic trade, and sailing vessels were increasingly confined to marginal trades. Nevertheless, they still had a role in moving low-value bulk cargoes and could still operate at a small profit by careful management. The *Charles Racine* found herself in Boston Harbor—and specifically at the Mystic River wharves—because a trade in American and Canadian lumber flourished between Boston and Argentina.

Her trade was not glamorous, but for O'Neill the *Charles Racine* would have represented the essence of the romantic era of the clipper ships, an era that was short-lived and more than 50 years in the past. Developed by American shipbuilders to rush cargoes home from China or out to California, the clippers had combined long, sleek hulls with towering masts and great expanses of sail. The clippers were first developed in the early 1840s and were disappearing by the start of the Civil War. About 450 American vessels fit the general characteristics of clipper ships during that period. Built a generation later, the *Charles Racine* was one of the efficient, iron-hulled square-riggers built late in the age of sail, combining a moderate rig with a capacious hull. These vessels could be operated with a much smaller crew than could the earlier clippers. And European iron and steel hulls were lighter and more durable than the wooden hulls of American square-riggers.

When James O'Neill met Captain Gustav Waage of the *Charles Racine* he felt confident his son would be in good hands, and a deal was arranged. In addition, a friend accompanied O'Neill on the trip. This friend has not been definitively identified, but Sheaffer speculates that it may have been Louis Holladay, O'Neill's friend from New York City.

Captain Waage was paid $75.00 for the fare (Sheaffer, SP, 161). In a letter to the ship's owners on 7 June 1910 Captain Waage wrote: "The passengers are two boys, who I have been asked to take care of, and it is understood that they are going to work on the voyage."[2]

It is possible that O'Neill signed on the ship as an Ordinary Seaman, since the *Charles Racine* was not licensed to carry passengers. It was a common practice to sign on non-crew members, including officers' wives, to avoid difficulties in foreign ports.[3] But even if they did sign the crew list the fact is that O'Neill and his friend were passengers who would do some work on the ship. They were not real seamen.

Spare hands would have been welcome. At the time it was difficult for a Norwegian sailing ship to acquire a crew in the United States, since American and British ships paid better and had shipping agents in port to help them find crew. Fewer and fewer men were interested in working on sailing ships, preferring the easier routine and more comfortable quarters on steamships. In his letter to the owners Waage wrote that he was "lucky enough to only pay blood money, $12, — , for one man only."[4] This was a fee to a shipping agent to find and provide a crew member. With sailing vessels fast becoming things of the past, O'Neill was fortunate to have found passage on the *Charles Racine*. It offered a unique challenge and a romantic view of a disappearing world.

CHARLES RACINE

"I lay on the bowsprit, facing astern, with the water foaming into spume under me, the masts with every sail white in the moonlight, towering high above me."
—Edmund, *Long Day's Journey into Night*

Eugene O'Neill had no way of knowing how formative an experience he was about to have when he joined the *Charles Racine*. It was June 1910. He was 21 years old. Both the ship and its captain were exceptional for their time. Captain Gustav Waage had convinced the Sigval Bergesen Line of Stavanger, Norway, to build the *Charles Racine,* a sailing vessel, in the early 1890s. At that time most of the vessels that the Bergesen Line owned and the new ones they were building were steamers. Captain Waage's experience and reputation as a sailing-ship captain swayed the Bergesen Line to accede to his wishes (Sheaffer, SP, 161). According to *Lloyd's Register*, the *Charles Racine* was launched in 1892, with Captain Waage as master. The vessel was 250.2 feet long with a breadth of 38.5 feet and depth of 22 feet. Lloyd's of London surveyed her twice during the building and again in

Captain Gustav Waage
(left) with his brother
and a passenger
on the quarterdeck
of the *Charles Racine*
(Sheaffer–O'Neill
Collection,
Connecticut College)

1904 and 1908, and issued their highest rating of 100 A1. The *Charles Racine* was a three-masted bark, which means that she carried square sails—sails that cross the line of the keel—on her foremast and mainmast, but on her mizzenmast she carried only fore-and-aft sails, which run along the line of the keel.

Captain Waage had a reputation throughout the maritime world for his efficiency in delivering cargo without loss or damage, a testament to his skill. He was known for fast passages, and he never spared anything to achieve this goal, demanding a great deal from his officers and crew, and also from himself. He loved to sail and had little respect for steamers, which "boiled themselves across oceans."[5]

Although she flew the Norwegian flag, the *Racine* was usually engaged in the lumber trade between Boston and Buenos Aires. Argentina had seen heavy investment and immigration from Britain and Europe in the late nineteenth century and experienced a boom at the turn of the century. As a result there was a high demand for lumber in Argentina, a country without its own timber resources. The ports of Boston and Portland, Maine, figured prominently as the providers. The return cargoes were wool and hides from the sheep and cattle that grazed on the pampas (Bunting, 378). A number of square-rigged vessels, sailing under a variety of flags, were involved in the trade up until 1914 because it was one of the few remaining routes where a profit could be made under sail.

O'Neill's passage from Boston to Buenos Aires, which began in early June and ended in early August of 1910, was one of the most difficult and slow trips Captain Waage had ever experienced. The voyage of 5,900 nautical miles took 57 days. By contrast, during another passage that year, the *Racine* sailed from Nova Scotia to Buenos Aires, a distance of 5,700 nautical miles, in 37 days (Sheaffer, SP 169).

With a large load of rough-cut timber filling her hold and chained down to the height of the rail on deck, the *Charles Racine* was towed free of the ships lining the Mystic Wharves and moved downstream, around Charlestown and into Boston Harbor. With a pilot on board she was then towed down between the islands of Boston Harbor as the crew went aloft to set sail. With her sails snapping as they were sheeted home and hoisted taut, the ship would have surged up to the towboat and dropped the towing hawser off Boston Light with a good breeze to push her across Massachusetts Bay and into the open ocean out beyond Cape Cod.

Aboard the *Charles Racine,* O'Neill was introduced to the community of ship life and developed memorable relationships with the men. Years later O'Neill spoke of the *Racine* crew: "They were fine fellows. I've never forgotten them, nor, I hope they me. Indeed, I look on a sailor man as my particular brother" (Sheaffer, SP, 167). The *Racine* had a crew of 19 men plus the captain and first and second mates. They were primarily Norwegian, but there were also Swedes, Finns, Germans, and Jamaicans. The crew complement included a sailmaker, carpenter, six Able Bodied Seamen, three Ordinary Seamen, four Youngmen (apprentices), two deck boys, a steward, and a cook.[6] As on any ship, the work continued around the clock. The crew was divided into two watches, with always one on deck while the other was off duty, generally in their quarters resting.

The carpenter, sailmaker, steward, and cook, referred to as daymen or idlers, were not part of a particular watch and worked only during the daylight hours, except in emergencies (Weibust, 49). Severin Waage, son of Captain Waage, sailed with his father on the voyages before and after O'Neill's trip. He said, based on his experience with his father when passengers were carried, that O'Neill probably did not have to work on board but helped out to pass the time.[7] O'Neill's work would have been during the day, leaving his evenings free to spend time observing.

O'Neill and his companion were quartered in a small cabin in the "half deck" on the port side aft and under the *Racine*'s quarterdeck. At other times the cabin had been used as a sickbay. It was small and cramped, but comfortable enough compared to the quarters for sailors of the time. Traditionally the crew lived forward, in the forecastle—fo'c's'le for short —the least comfortable area of a ship. The front end of the ship takes the greatest beating from the sea. By this time the fo'c's'le was a deckhouse aft of the foremast, with a bunkroom for each watch and usually the galley, plus cabins and workshops for the carpenter and sailmaker. The officers' quarters were in the stern, beneath the quarterdeck.

Crew aboard the *Charles Racine*, ca. 1910 (Sheaffer–O'Neill Collection, Connecticut College)

O'Neill took his meals with the officers in the after cabin, but the food was the same for everyone on board. It was typical sailors' fare—coffee, biscuits or bread, boiled beans or rice, salted or canned meat, salted fish, and dried vegetables. Combinations of these ingredients were turned into "lapskaus" (a meat stew from leftovers), fishballs, soup, or "Plukkfish" (creamed leftover salted or fresh fish).[8] Food on Norwegian vessels was sparse as the owners wanted to keep the costs down. For the first two weeks food might be fresh, but after that it was all preserved food.[9]

Work never stops on board ship, and it can be assumed that O'Neill had an opportunity to observe most of it and to assist in many of the tasks. Some required skills; others were necessary and monotonous. Crew members took hour-long turns at the wheel and on lookout at the bow. There was a constant battle with rust. The damp air and the sea continually corrode steel vessels. In good weather the men chipped the rust and repainted, shined the brass, sanded, and scrubbed the teak deck. The yards and sails were trimmed by hauling on lines on deck if the wind shifted. There was continual work in the rigging, replacing ratlines, which formed the ladder the crew used to climb aloft, and other pieces of the standing and running rigging. There was the setting and furling of sails as the wind and weather dictated.

For some of the work, particularly at the capstan and in setting some of the larger sails, chanteys were sung to coordinate the effort.[10] One of the apprentices on board with O'Neill, Rolf Skjorestad, recalled the singing of "Rolling Home," "Homeward Bound," "Blow the Man Down," "Blow Boys Blow," "Whiskey Johnny," and "Paddy Doyle's Boots."[11]

"Rolling Home" and "Homeward Bound" are capstan chanteys, long, melodic songs generally used when a crew was walking around the capstan to heave up the anchor. "Blow the Man Down," "Blow Boys Blow," and "Whiskey Johnny" are halyard chanteys used to coordinate the effort of the crew as they haul on a line on deck, called a halyard, to raise the yard and set a square sail. These shorter songs have choruses timed to help the men haul in unison. "Paddy Doyle's Boots" is a short chant of one verse used to flip the heavy weight of a rolled-up square sail onto the top of the yard as it is being furled.

O'Neill certainly would have had the opportunity to join in the singing of chanteys, as long as he was participating in the work. Chanteys appear in many of his plays, including "Whiskey Johnny" in *The Hairy Ape* and "Blow the Man Down" in *The Moon of the Caribbees.*

Except for the helmsman and the lookout, who were on duty, at night the crew on watch would be idle, standing by on deck in case they were needed. They usually congregated before the mainmast or on the main hatch to trade stories and sing.[12] Chanteys were rarely sung during a sailor's time off, because they were considered tools for work. But sailors sang popular tunes of the day, and some versions of the more melodic chanteys, such as "Rolling Home" and "Homeward Bound," might be sung during leisure time.

O'Neill, in all probability, was an eager listener, which encouraged the men to spin their yarns. He had the opportunity to hear the sailors' songs and stories of their adventures at sea and their exploits in port. He listened to their tales of happy and sad times, the people they missed and those they were glad to get away from, tales of shipwrecks, storms, shanghaiing, and distant lands. Seamen say that conversation in broad daylight is nothing like words spoken on board ship at night in the tropics or at sunset (Weibust, 136). The bonds that are created in such times are strong—something O'Neill would carry with him for years to come.

Sailors engaged in a number of other off-duty activities aboard ship. A popular one was fishing for bonito, albacore, dolphin fish, and occasionally shark.[13] Fishing was great sport, but it was also a source of fresh meat. On a relatively calm day men could climb out on the bowsprit and suspend a hook, tied with a red or white bow, and bob it up and down just above the water imitating the action of flying fish. Bonito, albacore, and dolphin fish like to play in the rush of the water at the bow. They leapt out of the water to the bait and were hauled in by the sailors.

Fishing for shark was a more challenging experience. The ship had to be in a calm sea with no wind. A large hook attached to a chain, with a piece of salt pork as bait, was dropped over the side. On one occasion aboard the *Charles Racine* when a shark was snared, it took seven men to pull the nine-foot shark on board. It flailed around with its tail sounding like a pistol shot as it slapped against the deck. When the shark was quiet one of the men cut off its tail, which was kept as a trophy.[14] Sailors hated sharks, and if they had the opportunity to kill one they would. Even though the meat of some sharks is white, delicate, and tastes good, many sailors were not interested in eating it. They believed that the shark had probably made a meal of an unlucky sailor somewhere (Hibberd, 9). Osmund Christophersen, the *Racine* deck boy, recalled O'Neill taking part in the catching of a shark. It was another colorful experience for the future playwright to remember.

A tradition on many deepwater sailing vessels was the "crossing-the-line ceremony," which was an initiation rite for sailors crossing the equator for the first time. The ceremony was described earlier in the discussion of the Jibboom Club in New London. There is no evidence that O'Neill went through such a ceremony on board the *Charles Racine.* This could be due to the fact that he did not live with the crew and was therefore not included in their rituals. Based on the many stories that O'Neill told friends and interviewers, it has to be assumed that had he experienced such an initiation he would have talked about it.

The *Charles Racine's* passage to Buenos Aires began well: "it took us 16 days to reach 8 [degrees] North Latitude," Captain Waage later reported. "We therefore thought that we were about to make record voyage."[15] The *Racine's* logbook entry for 15 June indicates that all sails were set and the ship was moving well at 12 knots (about 14 miles per hour). O'Neill recalls the speed and glory of sailing on a square-rigger in *Long Day's Journey into Night* as Edmond speaks to his father in Act Four. "The old hooker driving fourteen knots. I lay on the bowsprit, facing astern, with the water foaming into spume under me, the masts with every sail white in the moonlight, towering high above me" (O'Neill, CP3, 811). "Hooker" was a sailor's term of affection for a sailing vessel.

Captain Waage expected the normal wind pattern for the passage. In the North Atlantic, west and northwest winds would push them offshore and well south, with perhaps some unsettled weather as they crossed the warm Gulf Stream. After a fluky transitional stretch in the "Horse Latitudes" they would enter the trade winds, which blow from the east and southeast, pushing them well down to the equator. The calm equatorial stretch would be followed by the trade winds from the easterly to push them in to the Argentine coast. With the pushing power of their square sails, vessels like the *Racine* were well designed to ply the patterns of these steady winds. Unable to sail closer than 45 degrees into the direction of the wind, and requiring physical effort and coordination to change tacks (by which they swing through or away from the wind to bring it onto their other side), they were not well suited to sailing to windward or making frequent changes of direction.

What began so auspiciously then turned into an exceptionally difficult trip for Captain Waage and everyone on board, and certainly O'Neill, who would draw upon the recollection in his writing. The *Racine* experienced all types of weather. The ship's log recorded: "nice weather," "rain," "pouring rain," "lightning," "calm," and "hurricane." The *Racine's* log entry for 8 July stated: "Wind draw ahead to S.SW. Was obliged to tack SE ward. This is the first time in all the years I have been sailing southward. Nearly every year since 1868 I have been sailing here."[16] Waage was referring to the normally predictable trade winds, which had betrayed them.

Captain Waage reported that they fell into calms, which are generally encountered in the hotter regions. Rex Clements, who sailed as an apprentice aboard the Scottish bark *Arethusa* around 1900 and lived in quarters similar to O'Neill's, described the experience:

> We lay helpless on an oily sea, the spars sticking up idly into the still air. The heat grew terrific; bare iron was too hot to touch and the pitch bubbled out of the seams between the planking and stuck to our bare feet. From the yards the sails hung listlessly in heavy folds; we hauled the uselessly flapping mains'l up and listened to the grind and rasp of the parrels as she rocked to some imperceptible underrunning swell.
>
> It was exasperating. The men at the wheel leaned idly over the spokes, for she had lost steerage way; the half-deck was like a furnace and our only amusement was scanning the face of the brazen heavens and whistling for a wind (Clements, 54).

O'Neill experienced both the exhilaration and glory of sailing in the trade winds and the excruciating monotony of being becalmed. The next challenge was the terror of a storm at sea. The log of the *Charles Racine* gives a vivid description of an eight-day period of unpredictable events, beginning on 24 July: "Barometer constantly falling. Hurricane—storm from NW–W. Terrific heavy sea. At 4 o'clock only lower topsail on. Turned northward. Some deck cargo—planks—washed over."[17] The power of the sea sweeping across the deck and the pitching of the vessel broke the deck cargo free. The danger in such a situation is tremendous. Cargo loose on deck can create its own damage as it moves about and endangers the ship and the life of anyone on deck.

By the next day, 25 July, the wind began to decrease and by midday was calm. Over the course of the next four days the crew had to contend with weather that abated and then came at the ship from another direction. The level of the wind rose to storm force and then fell again to calm. During the periods of calm the crew set additional sails, only to have to furl those sails a short time later as the wind increased. In order to set, and particularly to furl, sails aboard a square-rigger, the crew had to go aloft into the rigging high above the deck and out onto the yards, from which the sails hung. In furling sails the sailors stand on footropes suspended along the length of the yards and lean over the yard to gather the sail and roll it into itself, all the while struggling against the wind's efforts to fill the sail. In a storm-tossed sea the ship is rising up on the peaks of the waves and then riding down into the troughs. In any storm it is important to keep some sail set so that the ship can maneuver itself, maintaining steerageway, and ride out the storm. The lower topsails (the second-lowest set of square sails) were the first to be set and the last to be furled. One or two staysails (fore-and-aft, triangular sails set on the supporting stays between the masts) were also used to provide stability during a storm.

The entry in the ship's log for 29 July stated: "wind increasing in force to hurricane [more than 73 miles per hour]. Made fast all sails except lower topsails. Put additional seizings on most of the sails. Violent hurricane squalls. Wishing lower topsails were made fast, let them stay, hoping that nothing should break. At noon the wind was moderating a little."[18] The entry for 30 July shows that one of the square sails was damaged and a staysail was lost in the storm.

The storm the *Charles Racine* encountered on 29 July, just outside of the Rio de la Plata, an estuary between Argentina and Uruguay, was probably a pampero of hurricane force.[19] Pamperos occur in the vicinity of the Rio de la Plata, deriving their name from the pampas of Argentina where they are generated by the hot north winds meeting the cold south polar winds (Weibust, 5). These sudden, brief storms sank or damaged many sailing vessels. J. S. Learmont experienced such a storm while on board the full-rigged ship *Brenhilda*:

The wind had been fresh to strong from the north west with heavy rain, and unsteady in force and direction. About midnight the darkness was "as black as the Earl of Hell's riding boots"; suddenly with a flash the whole sky lit up, the lightning making it a mass of fire. It was really terrifying. I hove her round, shortened sail and waited, and that wasn't long. It came out of the south west in a terrific squall, the deluge of rain drenching everyone. Even under only two topsails the *Brenhilda* lay down to the blast until her starboard rail was under water. In about six hours the pampero had blown itself out and the wind went into the westward. The suddenness of those storms is the danger; there is only lightning to warn you, the barometer cannot as they come down so quickly (Weibust, 6).

It is doubtful that Captain Waage would have allowed O'Neill aloft in any of the storms to help with the sails. But without question O'Neill was on deck in that hurricane-tossed sea, observing the crew struggling against the elements, which offered an emotional reminder of how small and insignificant a man is in the grand scheme of the earth and the elements. Osmund Christophersen, who had been deck boy aboard the *Charles Racine,* recalled seeing O'Neill and his friend watching the ravages of the storm. The next day Christophersen asked O'Neill what he had thought about the weather and O'Neill replied, "Very interesting, but I could have wished for less of it."[20]

The 57-day passage aboard the *Charles Racine* from Boston to Buenos Aires was filled with images and ideas that would linger in O'Neill's memory and appear later in some of his plays. The *Charles Racine* was the only square-rigged vessel on which O'Neill sailed, one of the last of a long line of ships from the glorious days of sail. On board the *Charles Racine,* O'Neill was introduced to and learned the ways of ships and sailors, knowledge he would put to use on other voyages. He was fortunate to have sailed with one of the most respected and experienced captains of his time. Stephen Black, who has written a psychoanalytical inquiry into O'Neill, says that by the end of O'Neill's voyage on the *Charles Racine* he had become a different person (Black, 107). It has been said that the best training ground for a sailor is a hard sea; a rough sea and storms "makes seamen of boys" (Weibust, 229).

BUENOS AIRES

"D'yuh remember the times we've had in Buenos Aires? The moving pictures in Barracas? Some class to them, d'yuh remember?"

—Yank, *Bound East for Cardiff*

Arriving off the broad mouth of the Rio de la Plata, the *Charles Racine* headed in, passing Montevideo, Uruguay, and continuing another 120 miles to reach the entrance to the expanding commercial port of Buenos Aires. Beyond the industrialized waterfront district the city of a million residents spread out in a grid pattern. Buenos Aires was a principal destination for European emigrants, so Italian, Russian, Polish, and even Arabic languages could be heard in the streets, mixed with the Spanish of native speakers.

But O'Neill experienced Buenos Aires as a sailor, not a tourist. Into the 1900s every large and medium-size port had a sailortown, a neighborhood near the wharves with a high concentration of businesses providing services to the sailor: boardinghouses, brothels, bars, shipping agents, chandlers, and seaman's aide societies. Some of the establishments were reputable, many were not.

A sailor's life is one of extremes—at sea he is isolated from the world; ashore, the world descends on him, catering to his whims, needs, and desires. Sailors' expenses are covered at sea. If they have just signed off a vessel, they have wages for the last couple of months or even a year. Businesses on shore eagerly await a fresh load of sailors. As soon as a vessel has docked, and in many instances even before, it is accosted by runners from shoreside establishments competing to entice sailors to come to their places of operation.

O'Neill had been exposed to the sailortowns of New London, New York, and Boston, but Buenos Aires in 1910 was his first experience as a sailor in sailortown, after the deprivations and isolation at sea aboard the *Charles Racine*. Stan Hugill, a deepwater sailor and author, referred to Buenos Aires as the most popular of eastern South American ports among the seafaring community around the turn of the century (Hugill, ST, 240). Severin Waage, son of Captain Waage and a captain himself, spoke of the docks of Buenos Aires in 1910 as full of nightclubs and the sound of many languages. He recalled the agents from different bordellos coming on board the ship and leaving their cards. One card read, "Come up to my house, plenty fun, perty girls, plenty dance, three men killed last night."[21] Waage described what it was like for young men to step ashore "hungry" after a long voyage, searching for and becoming embroiled in

Buenos Aires harbor, ca. 1910 (Mystic Seaport 1993.80.3)

adventures. He said that O'Neill would have met sailors of many different nationalities all looking for the same thing, ready to be greeted by people who wanted to show them the "real paradise ashore."[22]

Buenos Aires was not a safe place for sailors, or any transient man. Many disreputable elements preyed on sailors, who had no one to look out for them or notice if they were missing. The abuses were many, and the authorities often ignored them.

Some bars and boardinghouses engaged in crimping or shanghaiing. This method of providing crew for a vessel, involved either trickery or virtual kidnapping. Some sailors passed out from drinking too much or were knocked out by a blow to the back of the head or by a narcotic slipped into a drink—perhaps a "Mickey Finn," a concoction developed in the 1860s by a chemist named Michael Finnegan, who had moved from Chicago to San Francisco (Hugill, ST, 164). However they were rendered unconscious, they would awaken on board ship, stripped of their money and indebted to the ship for their first month's wages, which had been paid to the crimp who delivered them. With the expansion of maritime trade there, the predatory business of crimping reached its height in Buenos Aires around 1900.

One of the most infamous crimps in Buenos Aires was Tommy Moore, who ran a sailors' boardinghouse and pub called the Harbor Lights. He became known for shipping corpses. He would drag a corpse on board a ship and throw it in a bunk, telling the mate that the man would have a hangover when he woke up in the morning. The mate would not realize that the man was dead until the ship was at sea (Hugill, ST, 242–43). Alcohol was spilled on the corpse to add reality to the story, or a rat was sewn into the clothing to give the corpse some movement. Severin Waage wrote to O'Neill biographer Louis Sheaffer in 1958 after reading the Glencairn plays. He had noticed a reference to Tommy Moore in *Bound East for Cardiff* and told Sheaffer that he knew Tommy Moore well and confirmed that he was a boardinghouse master in Buenos Aires. He referred to him as a slave driver and said that he had heard that he shipped a dead man onboard with some drunken sailors.[23]

A rival of Tommy Moore's in Buenos Aires was "The Big Swede," a German crimp who shanghaied all nationalities, but particularly his fellow countrymen (Hugill, ST, 242–43). Sailors were normally supplied by more reputable shipping agents, but captains might resort to crimps if they were in a port where it was difficult to find crew or if they were short on time. It was a way of getting men, but risky if the crimp was disreputable. The fee they paid, referred to as "blood money," was generally equal to one month's wage for a sailor and sometimes an additional commission. Through most of the nineteenth century when a sailor signed on he received one month's wages in advance to outfit himself for the voyage.[24] In the case of shanghaiing the crimp would be the recipient of the advance, and the sailor ended up at sea without proper clothing.

When James Bisset's steamship was due to leave Buenos Aires in 1905, the officers discovered they were missing two stokers and three coal trimmers, all Liverpool Irishmen. They had "gone on the booze and had been shanghaied into other ships." After a few hours' delay the ship's agent engaged the services of a crimp who delivered five men, all Liverpool Irishmen, at $20.00 a head, having shanghaied them from other ships. Bisset reported that once their minds cleared from the liquor they did a fine job (Bisset, 63). In the neighborhoods he frequented, O'Neill would have encountered both crimps and shanghaiing during his stay in Buenos Aires. Though not crimped himself, he heard enough about the practice to include a classic tale of shanghaiing in *The Long Voyage Home.*

When he arrived in Buenos Aires, O'Neill had money. His father had given him $60.00 for expenses, which Captain Waage had kept for safety during the passage.[25] That was a large amount for anyone roaming the sailortown of Buenos Aires. Osmund Christophersen, one of the deck boys, claimed that O'Neill was robbed a few days after their arrival. Severin Waage commented: "There were men ashore much more dangerous than Tommy Moore. . . . But [O'Neill] was not the first to lose money and not the last. Lucky he was not killed on the docks."[26]

O'Neill enjoyed the bars near the docks and often ended up at the Sailor's Opera, patronized by sailors of many nationalities: English, French, Italian, Spanish, German, and Scandinavian. One of the attractions was an all-female ensemble of violinists. Their violins were stringless. An all-male ensemble or a solo pianist hidden behind a curtain provided the music. The girls, to add to their appeal, had no underwear beneath their short skirts (Sheaffer, SP, 173). O'Neill referred to the Sailor's Opera as a "Madhouse":

Pickled sailors, sure-thing race track touts, soused boiled-white shirt declasse Englishmen, underlings in the Diplomatic Service, boys darting around tables leaving pink and yellow cards directing one to red-plush paradises, and entangled in the racket was the melody of some ancient turkey trot banged out by a sober pianist. . . . But somehow a regular program was in progress. Every one present was expected to contribute something. If your voice cracked your head usually did, too. Some old sailor might get up and unroll a yarn, another might do a dance, or there would be a heated discussion between, say, Yankee and British sailors as to the respective prowess of their ships. And, if nothing else promised, "a bit of a harmless fight" usually could be depended upon as the inevitable star feature to round out the evening's entertainment (Sheaffer, SP, 174).

Charles Ashleigh, an English reporter for the *Buenos Aires Herald* who later became active with the Industrial Workers of the World in the United States, met O'Neill in Buenos Aires. Ashleigh recalled entering a seaman's cafe crowded with sailors speaking dozens of languages and sitting in the only seat available, which turned out to be next to O'Neill, who was alone. "I ordered a glass of beer, and listened to the music supplied by the mulatto pianist, pounding out popular tunes. Now and then some husky stoker or deck hand would rise, walk lumberingly and self consciously to the pianist's platform and full-throatedly bellow out some sea song" (Sheaffer, SP, 182). Frederick Hettman, who also befriended O'Neill, recalled going to see the show at the Casino with O'Neill. There were European performances of songs, trapeze, and dancing, and one night an American couple performed a sharpshooting act. On the mezzanine of the Casino, women operated bars for the patrons.[27]

Buenos Aires had more than just bars and nightclubs to entertain sailors. It had pornography; indeed, O'Neill's traveling companion found work in an establishment that made pornographic lantern slides.[28] Many newspaper stands sold "dirty books" and pornographic postcards. With the development of the cinema, "blue pictures" were being shown (Hugill, ST, 242). The waterfront district of Barracas, a suburb of Buenos Aires, was very popular because theaters showed pornographic films made in France and Spain. The theaters' main rooms were lined with curtained alcoves just big enough for a bed. Between films, prostitutes would offer themselves to the customers like "peanut or popcorn hawkers at ball games" (Sheaffer, SP, 176). O'Neill said to an interviewer, "Those moving pictures in Barracas were mighty rough stuff. Nothin' was left to the imagination. Every form of perversity was enacted, and, of course, sailors flocked to them." He added, "But, save for the usual exceptions, they were not vicious men. They were in the main honest, good-natured, unheroically courageous men trying to pass the time pleasantly" (Estrin, 67).

Years later, Robert Rockmore, a friend of O'Neill's in New York, said that when the normally well-spoken O'Neill recalled his days as a sailor, he took on a different persona, reverting back to the language that was used in the sailor bars, movies, and whorehouses of Buenos Aires (Sheaffer, SA, 267).

When O'Neill first arrived in Buenos Aires he slept aboard the *Charles Racine* some nights and at the Continental Hotel on others (Sheaffer, SP, 177). He returned to the ship for lunch and dinner. At the Continental Hotel, O'Neill met Frederick Hettman, an American working in Argentina as a surveyor. Hettman realized that O'Neill was the son of the famous actor, James O'Neill, and suggested that he and O'Neill room together in the hotel (Sheaffer, SP, 172), which they did for a time. O'Neill eventually moved to a less expensive boardinghouse, and for a short period he shared a room with a young Englishman named "Smitty," whom he had met at the Sailor's Opera. O'Neill described Smitty as a man of noble birth who had fallen into disgrace. O'Neill drew on his recollections of Smitty in his short story "Tomorrow" and the one-act play *In the Zone.*

While living at the boardinghouse, O'Neill worked at a few jobs. One was helping to unload the British square-rigged ship *Timandra,* which, like the *Racine,* was engaged in the lumber trade between Boston and Buenos Aires. O'Neill spoke of the experience: "that old bucko of a first mate was too tough, the kind that would drop a marlin spike on your skull from a yardarm" (Sheaffer, SP, 177).

O'Neill then found work tracing plans for an electrical supply firm. The work was well within his capabilities, but he found it too limiting and quit after a few weeks (Sheaffer, SP, 180). He next worked at the Swift Packing House, sorting raw hides. Cowhides and frozen beef were among

Argentina's most important exports. But the work, and especially the smell, were almost unbearable. Forty years later O'Neill described the experience to Hamilton Basso of *The New Yorker.* Basso wrote: "O'Neill still shudders when he recalls how the smell got into his clothes, his mouth, his eyes, his ears, his nose and his hair" (Sheaffer, SP, 184). Before O'Neill could quit, a fire destroyed the warehouse.

When O'Neill was out of work, he left the boardinghouse every day so that the landlady had the impression that he was working. Eventually his rent was so far in arrears that he was about to be thrown out. O'Neill contacted his friend Hettman, who paid the landlady two months' rent in advance (Sheaffer, SP, 180). Shortly afterwards Hettman left for the interior on a surveying trip. When he returned to Buenos Aires he visited the boardinghouse looking for O'Neill.

According to the landlady, O'Neill had left on a cattle boat for South Africa. Although later in life he claimed that he had made a round-trip voyage to Durban, South Africa, on a cattle steamer, there is no evidence that O'Neill actually sailed to South Africa. No legal document records that trip. Sheaffer's research also shows that no cattle steamer made such a passage during the time that O'Neill was in Buenos Aires (Sheaffer, SP, 183). Sheaffer suggests that O'Neill was in need of money to support his drinking so he told the landlady that he had work that was taking him away from Buenos Aires and convinced her to give him the balance of the rent back (Sheaffer, SP, 184).

Instead of setting out for South Africa, O'Neill lived "on the beach" or, more precisely, slept on the benches at the Paseo Colon, with other transients, using what little money he had to buy alcohol. In 1920, O'Neill told Olin Downes of the *Boston Sunday Post,* "I hadn't any job at all, and was down on the beach—'down,' if not precisely 'out'" (Estrin, 9). He sank into deep depression, falling so low that he reached a level of tranquility and knew he could fall no lower. In *Mourning Becomes Electra,* he gives voice to the experience through Orin: "you get so deep at the bottom of hell there is no lower you can sink and you rest in peace" (O'Neill, CP2, 1037). It was after languishing in Buenos Aires for seven months and hitting bottom that O'Neill pulled himself together enough to secure a situation aboard a ship bound for New York.

SS *IKALA*

"This sailor life ain't much to cry about leavin'—
just one ship after another, hard work, small pay, and bum grub;
and when we git into port, just a drunk endin' up in a fight,
and all your money gone, and then ship away again."

—Yank, *Bound East for Cardiff*

O'Neill's next experience at sea was aboard the SS *Ikala*, a British tramp freighter bound for New York from Buenos Aires. Tramp designates a vessel that has no specific route, with its itinerary dictated by the cargoes it secures and their destinations. In March 1911, as the *Ikala* prepared to leave for New York, it was short on crew so the captain took on "scenery bums," transients who joined the ship to get from one place to another (Sheaffer, SP, 185). O'Neill came on in this capacity: a working passenger.

The accepted truth has been that O'Neill was a crew member on the *Ikala*. The reality is that he was a passenger with the same status that he had on the *Charles Racine*. The details of O'Neill's signing on, and especially his signing off, the *Ikala* are particularly interesting. The "Agreement and Account of the Crew of the SS *Ikala*" states that "E. G. O'Neill," age 22, whose home was New York City, and whose first ship was the *Ikala,* signed on in Buenos Aires on 20 March 1911 as an Ordinary Seaman with a wage of one shilling a month.[29] In signing the document O'Neill stated that this was his first ship, confirming that aboard the *Charles Racine* he was a passenger. The admission that the *Ikala* was his first ship was made by O'Neill himself and contradicted his later claims that he was a member of the *Charles Racine's* crew. Also, saying that this was his first ship confirmed that the cattle boat to South Africa was a fabrication.

O'Neill's pay of one shilling a month was low for a seaman at the time. The same document shows a Mary Carruthers, presumably the wife of the *Ikala's* Captain Carruthers, signing on as stewardess, also to receive one shilling a month. Stewardesses served on steamers, but generally only when the vessel carried passengers, which the *Ikala* was not licensed to do. The Registrar General's Office of the Ministry of Transport and Civil Aviation of Great Britain interpreted the low wage as an indication that O'Neill was a passenger and not an actual crew member.[30] Since the *Ikala* was not licensed to carry passengers, the only way the vessel could carry them without the danger of violating its licensing was to sign those individuals on as crew members.

The *Ikala,* whose home port was Liverpool, was built in 1901 with the original name *Planet Neptune.* The name change came about with a change of ownership in 1909. Nothing in particular set the *Ikala* apart from other British freighters of the period. They were all of the same basic design and size (Sheaffer, SP, 184–85). It was a "three island" vessel type, meaning it had a raised forecastle head at the bow, a midship house, and a raised poop deck at the stern, giving it a profile of three islands raised above the deck (Bisset, 57–58). With a length of 385 feet the *Ikala* was considerably larger than the *Racine.* Constructed of steel, it was a single-screw steamer with one stack and two masts for cargo-handling, under the command of Captain R. Carruthers (Lloyd's, n.p.).

The operation of the *Ikala* was very different from that of the *Racine* and widened O'Neill's experience dramatically. Louis Sheaffer describes the contrast as poetry and prose. The *Racine* was the experience of the "collaboration of wind and sail and ocean," while the *Ikala* was simply the seagoing essence of "dull labor" (Sheaffer, SP, 185). But with regular food, a regular routine, and the absence of alcohol, O'Neill's time

The tramp steamer *Planet Neptune,* which was renamed the SS *Ikala* in 1909, was the inspiration for O'Neill's "SS *Glencairn.*" O'Neill sailed on the *Ikala* in 1911 from Buenos Aires to New York (Sheaffer-O'Neill Collection, Connecticut College)

on the *Ikala* was an improvement from the life he had been leading "on the beach" in Buenos Aires.

The *Ikala* departed Buenos Aires on 21 March 1911, with a deck crew of 15 men of English, Swedish, Russian, and Danish origin (Sheaffer, SP, 186). The deck crew was responsible for all the operation and maintenance above decks, duties that were considerably fewer on a steamer than on a sailing vessel. The need for traditional seamanship that had been common on sailing ships was almost nonexistent on steamships (Bisset, 16). The work primarily consisted of steering (reserved for Able Bodied Seamen), standing lookout, chipping rust, painting, scrubbing the deck, and, if the rare occasion arose, handling the limited sail that was carried. The deck crew was divided into two watches, four hours on and four off.

Many of the crew were stokers or firemen, who shoveled coal into the furnaces, and trimmers, who brought coal to the stokers. They worked four hours on and eight hours off. A steward, cook, carpenter, and lamp trimmer rounded out the crew. The lamp trimmer was an Able Bodied Seaman responsible for keeping the ship's running lights lit. The Lamp Trimmer quite often had the nickname of "Lamps" or "Lampy" (Bisset, 21). The officers included the captain, two mates for the deck crew, and engineering officers to supervise in the machinery spaces. The seamen, stokers, and trimmers all lived in the fo'c's'le, while the rest, including the officers, lived in the deckhouse below the bridge (Bisset, 16). O'Neill's living quarters on the *Ikala* were different from those on the *Charles Racine*. On the *Ikala* he lived with the crew.

Living in the fo'c's'le is very likely where O'Neill learned about the trust and respect that sailors had for each other. Sailors would come on board a vessel with their gear stored in a sea chest or seabag. The chest or bag contained their hand tools, clothing, foul weather gear, and any other personal items, which might include letters, pictures, or mementos of loved ones and souvenirs from various ports. An experienced sailor never locked his seabag or chest. It would signal that he questioned the trust of his fellow shipmates, and the feeling would be returned. Trust among shipmates was vital onboard ship, particularly in the age of sail. The work aloft in the rigging could be extremely dangerous, with men routinely putting their lives in the hands of their co-workers. If a sailor displayed his distrust by locking his sea chest, then the rest of the crew might believe that he would not trust them with his life, and therefore they could not trust him with theirs.

A locked chest provoked strong emotions. Shipmates might display their feelings by nailing the sea chest shut to insure that no one got into the chest, or each time they passed, give the lock a good kick until it broke. An inexperienced man soon learned that he needed to trust his fellow shipmates. O'Neill would reveal his understanding of trust among sailors in his one-act play, *In the Zone.*

The most essential crew onboard steamships were the stokers. They actually generated the power to make the ship move by feeding the furnaces, taking away from the Able Bodied Seaman what little prestige they had. The seamen no longer had the distinction of actively contributing to the propulsion of the ship and were reduced to general maintenance workers. James Bisset, who worked as third mate on the SS *Rembrandt,* a British tramp freighter similar to the *Ikala,* described the stokers and trimmers as "Liverpool Irish" who "were all tough looking characters, who worked in the stoke hold in dungarees, hobnail boots, and flannel shirts, with a sweat rag round their necks, and came up on deck, clambering out of the fiddlery [a hatchway] like demons out of hell, grimy and sweaty, for an occasional breath of fresh air, or to go forward off watch" (Bisset, 19). O'Neill drew on experiences like this as he wrote *The Hairy Ape.*

In 1940 O'Neill vividly recalled some of his experiences onboard the *Ikala* in a letter to Dudley Nichols, the screenwriter for the film *The Long Voyage Home,* which combined a few of the Glencairn plays.

> And here's a memory. When due for a crow's nest watch in a storm, the man about to relieve would wait in the door of the forecastle alleyway while a wave dashed over the forecastle head. Then as the wave receded down the deck, timing it just right, he would sprint for the ladder up the mainmast to the crow's nest—the idea being to get there and start climbing before the next sea came over and caught him.[31]

After two weeks on her passage to New York the *Ikala* stopped at Port of Spain, Trinidad. The arrival and departure of the ship was recorded in the *Port of Spain Gazette*'s shipping news column. On 7 April 1911, the arrivals column reported "Apr. 5—*Ikala,* Brit. Stmr., Carruthers, 2,821 tons, 16 days Buenos Aires, ballast (for bunker coal)," and on 8 April 1911 the departures column posted: "7th April—*Ikala,* Brit. Stmr., Carruthers, 2,821 tons, —New York, 555 bags Trinidad coconuts, 250 tons bunker coal—no passengers" (Sheaffer-O'Neill Collection). The harbor of Port of Spain was too shallow for the *Ikala* so the ship had to anchor about a half-mile away from the jetties while the cargo and coal were brought out in lighters (Sheaffer, SP, 187). It was the custom in many ports for vendors to go out to the ships to sell their wares—anything from souvenirs and fruits, vegetables, and fowl, to smuggled alcohol. A captain and his officers never wanted alcohol in the hands of the crew. It reduced their productivity and generally instigated fights. O'Neill reflected on this kind of situation in *The Moon of the Caribbees.*

The *Ikala* steamed from Trinidad to New York, arriving on 15 April, less than a month after its departure from Buenos Aires and almost a full year from when O'Neill had left the United States aboard the *Charles Racine.* The *Ikala*'s crew list certifies that O'Neill deserted the ship in New York, forfeiting his wages. The only explanation for the charge of desertion is that O'Neill and Captain Carruthers never intended there to be an official relationship. It was customary aboard steamships that crew were signed off when they arrived in their home port (Bisset, 18). Since New York was O'Neill's home, there was no reason for him to desert the ship. Also, there was no need for the captain of the *Ikala* to keep O'Neill on as crew, since in New York crews were readily available. The captain had to record that O'Neill deserted; otherwise O'Neill would have officially remained as part of the ship's complement. In 1911 the only penalty for desertion from a merchant ship was the forfeiture of wages and belongings left on board. Prior to 1895 desertion had the added penalty of imprisonment (Wissman, 140–41). The only logical interpretation for O'Neill leaving the *Ikala* without signing off (desertion) is that he did not expect wages and, by his desertion, the captain was not legally bound to pay any wages. The whole scenario of the *Ikala* leads to the conclusion that O'Neill was primarily a passenger and he was using the *Ikala* to make his way home to New York.

Four other individuals listed in the Agreement and Account of Crew for the SS *Ikala* signed on at the same rate as O'Neill and also deserted in New York. One, presumably a friend of O'Neill's, signed on in Buenos Aires at the same time and date as O'Neill, and three others signed on in

Trinidad. The other crewmen listed in the Agreement and Account of Crew signed on at a reasonable going rate of pay and either stayed with the vessel or officially signed off and received their pay.[32] This information leads one to conclude that those crew members who earned a reasonable rate were official members of the crew and those that were listed as earning a shilling a month were not official crew members in the eyes of the captain and ship owners.

The time O'Neill spent on the *Ikala* was short, but the experiences he had aboard the steamer were the source of his ideas for the Glencairn plays and other longer works. In O'Neill's year away from the familiar world of his family, he had sailed aboard a windjammer and a steamer—two contrasting adventures that expanded his view of the world and himself, and left him with a storehouse of images that would inspire him when he settled down to write.

NEW YORK

"I shared a small rear room with another 'gentleman-ranker,' . . .
over an all-night dive near South Street known as Tommy the Priest's."
—"Tomorrow"

On his arrival in New York, O'Neill made contact with his father, who was about to go out on tour. His father gave O'Neill an allowance of $7.00 per week, which he had to collect in person from his father's business associate, George C. Tyler (Black, 112). Obviously, James O'Neill wanted a way to keep track of his son.

O'Neill drifted back to New York's sailortown and settled at a sailors' flophouse and bar called Jimmy the Priest's, at 252 Fulton Street, opposite Washington Market, a few doors down from West Street. The building that housed Jimmy the Priest's and others in the neighborhood were later torn down to make way for the World Trade Center.

Jimmy the Priest's was in the heart of sailortown, in a red-brick building that was about a hundred years old at the time. Four and a half stories tall, it was an unexceptional commercial block building. The front window had a sketch of a large beer glass and in faded letters "schooner—

252 Fulton Street (ca. 1920), the location of Jimmy the Priest's, the saloon and sailors' flophouse where O'Neill lived on and off in 1911 and 1912 (Sheaffer-O'Neill Collection, Connecticut College)

5 [cents]." Inside on the old mahogany bar, sailors could find a free lunch of simple foods to go with their beer. A rear room contained round tables, chairs, and a pot-bellied stove. A curtain could be drawn to separate the two rooms (Sheaffer, SP, 189). According to Stan Hugill, such places were common in New York's sailortown around the turn of the century (Hugill, ST, 158–59).

O'Neill was apparently attracted to Jimmy's for its inexpensive drinks of relatively good quality. Whiskey could be had for 5 cents, as could a 16-ounce schooner of beer. Other places charged ten cents for a 12-ounce stein of beer. Jimmy's stayed open later than the other bars and had a flophouse upstairs where O'Neill was able to rent a room for $3.00 a month (Estrin, 68). The rooms, or more accurately cells, were located on the second and third floors. They lined the walls with a single aisle down the center. Each of the windowless cells was equipped with a cot, straw mattress, and chair. The cells were divided by partitions, with wire mesh covering the top and a flimsy lockable door to discourage anyone from disturbing tenants' belongings. There was only one kerosene light on each floor. These were far from plush surroundings, but, for men who had come from ships, the conditions were not a far cry from what they were used to. Every day at noon Jimmy put out a free lunch, which featured a large pot of soup. Most of his customers who came in for a drink ignored the lunch, but his boarders and some others depended on it. Even if they were out of money to buy drinks, Jimmy would let them have a bowl or two (Sheaffer, SP, 191–92).

Few of his patrons knew that Jimmy the Priest's real name was James J. Condon. He was about 50 when O'Neill met him. Condon had run other bars on West Street before moving to the Fulton Street location in 1908. Two men who had worked at the chandlery next door to Jimmy's recalled him as a fearless man. The moment he expected trouble from a customer Jimmy grabbed the offender and threw him out the door into the street, never looking to see if he had been hurt on the stone steps or in the street. But he also had a soft side. He would help a drunken sailor down on his luck by letting him board in the rooms upstairs, and he was known for not crimping any of his customers. He also never interfered with any of his regulars when they followed a drunken transient out into the street with the intent to fleece him of his money or belongings (Sheaffer, SP, 189–90).

O'Neill described the clientele at Jimmy's as a "hard lot, at first glance. Every type; sailors on shore leave or stranded; longshoremen, waterfront riffraff, gangsters, down and outers, drifters from the ends of the earth. . . . They were sincere, loyal and generous. In some queer way they carried on. I learned at Jimmy the Priest's not to sit in judgment on people" (Sheaffer, SP, 192).

In an interview that appeared in *American Magazine* in 1922, when O'Neill was 34, he told Mary B. Mullett:

> I liked [sailors] better than I did men of my own kind. They were sincere, loyal, generous. You have heard people use the expression: 'He would give away his shirt.' I've known men who actually did give away their shirts. I've seen them give their own clothes to stowaways. I hated a life ruled by conventions and traditions of society. Sailors' lives, too, were ruled by conventions and traditions; but they were of a sort I liked and that had a meaning which appealed to me (Estrin, 33–35).

The area around Jimmy's was busy at night and in the early morning with the comings and goings at Washington Market. In 1909 New York City invested $52,000 into improvements in the market, which had been established in 1812. Just before the First World War, the market's annual business exceeded 4.5 million dollars and directly and indirectly fed a million people a day (Witmore, 35). In addition to the market, the area bustled with the businesses and industry in lower Manhattan, riverfront commerce, commuter ferries, and a little farther north the oceangoing steamship companies. The activity in the neighborhood generated an ample supply of customers for the local prostitutes—farmhands from the market, sailors, and roustabouts. When he tired of the lively surroundings, O'Neill escaped to the Battery to sit in the sun and watch the traffic in the harbor (Sheaffer, SP, 192).

AMERICAN LINE

"I was lookout on the crow's nest in the dawn watch. . . .
The passengers asleep and none of the crew in sight. No sound of
man. Black smoke pouring from the funnels behind and beneath me."
—Edmund, *Long Day's Journey into Night*

After three months at Jimmy the Priest's in New York's sailortown, O'Neill was drawn to sea again. He signed on the transatlantic passenger steamer SS *New York* of the American Line as an Ordinary Seaman, departing on 22 July 1911 for Southampton, England (Sheaffer, SP, 194). This was O'Neill's first passage as a paid seaman.

The American Line began its service between New York and Southampton in 1893 and was the first passenger line to do so. The passage of the Postal Aid Act of 1891 paved the way for the American Line's initial success. The company was awarded the contract to carry mail to England, which required regular weekly service (Flayhart, 137). Up until that time most of the passenger lines went into Liverpool. Located on the south coast of England rather than up the Irish Sea, Southampton was easier to navigate into and ships did not have to wait for high tide to dock as they did in Liverpool. Direct railway service from Southampton to

The American Line's SS *New York* is shown in New York harbor in 1895, before the ship was outfitted with new engines and only two stacks. (Mystic Seaport 1988.96.3)

London was added to accommodate the American Line passengers, which enabled them to arrive in London two hours after disembarking. In New York, the American Line built a new pier and passenger terminal on the west side of Manhattan, located between Fulton and Vesey Streets, not far from Jimmy the Priest's. When they were built, the terminal and the pier—named Washington Pier, but more commonly referred to as Pier 14—were the largest in New York. The terminal was the first of its kind with two stories. The lower level was for cargo and provisioning and the second level was reserved for passengers. For the first time, passengers were able to walk directly onto the ship and were separated from the dirt associated with the loading of cargo and provisions. The new accommodations for passengers, the ease of docking, which helped to reduce travel time, and Southampton's proximity to the British capital and the rest of Europe provided the American Line with great advantages over its competitors. By 1910, both of the American Line's major competitors, the Cunard and White Star Lines, had shifted their operations from Liverpool to Southampton.

The American Line's first ship to arrive in Southampton was the SS *New York*. The line operated two principal steamers on opposing schedules. The 527-foot *New York* had been built as the *City of New York* at Glasgow in

1888 and transferred to American registry through the postal act. Her similar sister, *Philadelphia,* had been launched the same year as the *City of Paris.* They were the first two modern American passenger liners, though after 20 years of service they were outclassed by newer and larger European liners.

O'Neill's standing with the American Line was indeed different from his role on board the *Ikala.* "The Shipping Register for SS *New York*" shows him signing on in New York on 17 July 1911, in the capacity of Ordinary Seaman at a rate of $27.50 per run. (A run is a passage from one place to the next.)

The *New York* was considerably larger than either the *Charles Racine* or the *Ikala,* and differed in others ways as well. The *New York* was a passenger ship, while the other ships on which O'Neill sailed were cargo-carrying freighters. The *New York* could carry 1,290 passengers: 290 in first class, 250 in second class, and 750 in steerage—the area usually accommodating immigrants (Miller, 47). The crew, which totaled nearly 400, was cramped in small quarters. Their food—typical sailor's fare of salted and canned meats and beans—contrasted greatly with that of the passengers (Sheaffer, SP, 194).

According to O'Neill, "there was about as much 'sea glamour' in working aboard a passenger steamship as there would have been in working in a summer hotel! I washed enough deck area to cover a good-sized town" (Estrin, 30).

O'Neill did not mind the work on board the *New York,* but he resented the passengers, who lounged and promenaded around the decks while he was on his hands and knees scrubbing. The extremity of the contrast between O'Neill's place on board ship and that of the passengers destroyed his image of the heroic sailor whom he had come to know and admire. Aboard a steamship, the sailor, once challenged by and becoming one with nature and the elements, was reduced to the role of a cleaning servant. O'Neill later would give vent to this resentment in the play *The Hairy Ape* when, in frustration, Yank lashes out at the heiress.

Aboard the *New York,* as on the *Ikala,* O'Neill came face-to-face with the changing technology of the times. Steam was in command of the seas. The age of sail was at the end of its decline. O'Neill encountered the animosity that existed between seamen and the "black gang," the

Passengers on board the American Line's SS *New York*, ca. 1905, on which O'Neill sailed from New York to Southampton in 1911 with the rank of Ordinary Seaman (Mystic Seaport 1994.10.3)

name given to firemen or stokers and trimmers. The black gang looked down on the seamen as weaklings and part of the past, while the seamen viewed the black gang as subhuman (Sheaffer, SP, 194).

The work of the black gang was mechanical. The American Line ships *New York* and *Philadelphia* had each been refitted with new high-pressure, triple-expansion steam engines at the turn of the century. To produce the superheated steam to drive these engines, the ships' boilers consumed about 13 tons of coal per hour. Trimmers trundled the coal from the storage bunkers in wheelbarrows and carried away the ashes. The firemen or stokers shoveled the coal into the furnaces, trimmed the fire with a slice bar, and shook the grates to remove the ashes. Despite the physical requirements of their job, stokers were skilled practitioners of fire, able to gauge its quality by the color and sound of the burning coal. They fed the furnaces and took instructions from engineers, who ran the engines, while communicating with the officers on the bridge by way of bells or whistles.

An article in the 13 July 1912 edition of the *New London Telegraph*—a month before O'Neill began working for the paper—describes the stokehold and work that went on there:

> An inferno, all smoke and heat and fire and nakedness, is the stoke hole [sic] of an ocean liner. As you enter it, picking your way over the burning ashes, the hot blast from the furnace mouths smites you in the face; it scorches your eyes and sears your lungs with every gasping breath you draw. . . .
>
> And yet the inferno hums with life and strenuous, almost savage, industry. Opposite the huge boilers, quivering with suppressed power, like so many chained giants, are the figures of men as if carved in ebony, glistening with the sweat that streams from every pore. They are working furiously, with muscles swelling and knotting as if they would burst through [the] skin. . . . Gathering up a shovelful of coal, each man propels them [the coals] with a quick forward thrust of the body into the white hot heart of the furnace and with a dexterous turn of the wrist spreads them evenly over the fire. Then, quick as the eye can follow, another shovel full succeeds and another (Sheaffer, SP, 194–95).

It was not uncommon for trimmers or firemen to be overcome by the heat and exertion of their labors. If the crew in the stokehold was reduced by more than a third, or if there were a number of inexperienced men, then the speed of the ship was adversely affected. The success of the American Line rode on regular quick passages. It took several voyages for members of the black gang to adjust to the backbreaking and intense pace of the stokehold and become an efficient part of the machinery (Flayhart, 311). O'Neill would illustrate his awareness of the stress and strain of the stokehold in *The Hairy Ape*.

The seamen from the age of sail had to confront the changing conditions of the weather and adapt with a level of creativity, craftsmanship, and beauty in their work. Aboard steamers the work of seamen was stripped of challenge and detail, devoid of craftsmanship and creativity. It destroyed their pride. In contrast, the black gang took pride in their strength and endurance and in their contribution to the lifeblood of the ship.

The trip across the North Atlantic to England can be a treacherous one at any time of year. On a number of occasions aboard the *New York*,

The SS *Philadelphia*, ex. *City of Paris*, ca. 1910, the American Line ship on which O'Neill sailed from Southampton to New York in 1911 with the rank of Able Bodied Seaman (Mystic Seaport 1993.123.210

the glass dome skylight over some of the passenger areas on the top deck was smashed by furious seas, damaging furniture and carpets. Stewards would have to seal off the flooded passenger areas for the rest of the trip (Miller, 47). The passage from New York to Southampton normally took a week, but the *New York* developed engine trouble and arrived a day late. Most of the passengers disembarked at Southampton. Then the *New York* took its regular short run across the English Channel to Cherbourg, France, discharged its remaining passengers, and returned to Southampton and the dry dock for repairs (Sheaffer, SP, 195).

While the *New York* was in dry dock, O'Neill lived in Southampton and had the opportunity to get the feel of the British port. At the time, England was in the throes of the Great General Strike of 1911. At the center of the strike were the dock laborers and transport workers, joined by the stokers and seamen who put aside their differences and pledged their support for the strike. The railroads stopped running, and all ships were stuck in port. With the country's transportation system paralyzed, cities ran low on food. The strike activities in Southampton were relatively quiet compared to other ports, such as Liverpool.

Driscoll, a stoker from the American Line steamer SS *Philadelphia* was also in Southampton at the time, and O'Neill was greatly influenced by him. Driscoll had been born in Ireland, but O'Neill referred to him as a

Liverpool Irishman. According to O'Neill, Liverpool Irishmen were from families that "years ago . . . settled in Liverpool. Most of them followed the sea, and they were a hard lot. To sailors all over the world a 'Liverpool Irishman' is the synonym for a tough customer" (Sheaffer, SP, 196). O'Neill spoke to a reporter from the *New York Times* about Driscoll and said "He was a giant of a man, and absurdly strong. He thought a whole lot of himself, was a determined individualist. He was very proud of his strength, his capacity for grueling work. It seemed to give him mental poise to be able to dominate the stoke hold, to do more work than any of his mates" (Estrin, 67). O'Neill held Driscoll in very high regard and thought him a heroic figure. Driscoll would inspire many of O'Neill's theatrical characters, most notably Yank in *The Hairy Ape*.

When the strike ended, O'Neill secured the position of Able Bodied Seaman on board the *Philadelphia*. It is unclear if O'Neill obtained the position with Driscoll's assistance or through the offices of the American Line. Since he was still with the company while the *New York* was in dry dock, he may simply have been reassigned. When the *Philadelphia* departed Southampton for New York on 19 August 1911 (Sheaffer, SP, 197), Eugene O'Neill was on board as an Able Bodied Seaman. His duties were similar to those of an Ordinary Seaman—washing the decks and shifting baggage and mail—but included the additional duty of standing an occasional two-hour watch in the crow's nest. This assignment was a particular favorite of O'Neill's, (Sheaffer, SP, 197) and he would recount his experience in the crow's nest in *Long Day's Journey into Night*:

> on the American Line, when I was lookout on the crow's nest in the dawn watch. A calm sea, that time. Only a lazy ground swell and a slow drowsy roll of the ship. The passengers asleep and none of the crew in sight. No sound of man. Black smoke pouring from the funnels behind and beneath me. Dreaming, not keeping lookout, feeling alone, and above, and apart, watching the dawn creep like a painted dream over the sky and sea which slept together. Then the moment of ecstatic freedom came (O'Neill, CP3, 812).

O'Neill signed off the *Philadelphia* in New York City on 26 August 1911, which would prove to be the end of his career as a sailor. O'Neill was with the American Line for only four weeks. The document also indicates that he was transferred to the SS *Philadelphia* on 19 August 1911.[33] His pay rate was comparable to the other seamen signed on in the same capacity. The documents for "Mutual Release for the Crew of the SS *Philadelphia*," dated 26 August 1911, show that O'Neill signed off, his station was Able Bodied Seaman, and he received $14.84 in pay.[34] That O'Neill received pay for the passage and signed the Mutual Release is proof that he was a bona fide member of the crew. The discrepancy in the final pay is probably due to the fact that O'Neill had drawn from his wages. It was common practice for a sailor to have credit against his pay with the shipping company while he was in their employ.

That O'Neill's rank changed when he shifted from the *New York* to the *Philadelphia* was probably the result of proving that he knew his responsibilities aboard ship, knowledge derived from his experiences aboard the *New York* and as a working passenger on the *Charles Racine* and *Ikala*. O'Neill learned the duties of a seaman as had most seamen before him—by doing the work. Seamen learned by trial and error, imitation and demonstration, with threats and warnings from the officers to encourage them, and occasionally some actual instruction (Weibust, 218–20).

His time with the American Line, and earning the rank of Able Bodied Seaman, meant a great deal to Eugene O'Neill. He kept the certifi-

O'Neill's Certificate of Discharge, denoting his rank of AB, from the American Line's SS *Philadelphia*, 10 August, 1911 (Yale Collection of American Literature, Beinecke Rare Book and Manuscript Library, Yale University)

cate stating his rank as a prized possession throughout his life. Another cherished keepsake was a black sweater, part of his uniform from the American Line, which the crew wore coming and going from port. Twenty years later, O'Neill's wife Carlotta found the sweater and had it darned and presented it to her husband as a gift. According to Carlotta, O'Neill was very moved, referring to the sweater as being from the days when he was free (Sheaffer, SP, 197).

THE RETURN TO JIMMY THE PRIEST'S

"Gimme a whiskey—ginger ale on the side.
And don't be stingy, baby."
—Anna, *"Anna Christie"*

On his return from England in August of 1911, O'Neill settled in at Jimmy's again. Occasionally he went to the docks to find work as a long-shoreman loading and unloading ships, but most of the time he drank his money away at Jimmy's and other sailortown bars (Sheaffer, SP, 200). Driscoll, O'Neill's stoker friend from the American Line, went to Jimmy's with him, but he only stayed for a few days between passages of American Line ships. When Driscoll was in port he would return to Jimmy's with shipmates for several days of drink, song, and trading stories (Sheaffer, SP, 204).

At Jimmy's, O'Neill widened his circle of seafaring friends. Among them was Chris Christopherson, who worked on coastal coal barges. Born on the southern coast of Norway 40 years earlier, Christopherson had come from a long line of sailors and had shipped out at the age of 14 on a sailing vessel owned by a relative. By the time he was 22 he had become a mate. Although his seafaring was now centered on the east coast of North America, he had a wife and six children at home in Norway and returned every third year for an extended visit. Like Driscoll, Christopherson took to O'Neill and shared many details of life bound to the sea.

O'Neill later recalled that Christopherson "had followed the sea so long that he got sick at the thought of it . . . he spent his time getting drunk and cursing the sea. 'Dat ole davil,' he called it. Finally he got a job

Chris Christopherson ca.1910. O'Neill's friend from Jimmy the Priest's, he was the inspiration for Chris in *Chris Christophersen* and *"Anna Christie."* (Sheaffer–O'Neill Collection, Connecticut College)

as captain of a coal barge" (Sheaffer, SP, 202). The crew of a coal barge might number nine on a 300-foot barge like the *W. A. Thompson* on which Christopherson sailed.[35] The crew tended the lines in docking and getting underway, kept watch at the towing hawser during coastal passages, set sail on the barge, monitored the hold to make sure the coal cargo did not combust spontaneously, and did maintenance around the vessel. Christopherson pursued the life for another six years after meeting O'Neill. Then, on 22 October 1917, his body was found floating in New York Harbor off Liberty Island. Based on his knowledge of the man, O'Neill believed "he got terribly drunk and tottered away about 2 o'clock in the morning for his barge. . . . In the trying to board the barge he stumbled on the plank and fell over" (Estrin, 68). Christopherson was 47.

While O'Neill was living in the world of his seafaring friends at Jimmy's he did keep abreast of the theater world in the city. In November 1911, George C. Tyler brought the Abbey Players from Dublin to New York for a six-week run. Their repertoire of 16 plays included work by William Butler Yeats, John Millington Synge, Lady Augusta Gregory, and T. C. Murray. The productions did not draw much of an audience but O'Neill attended as many as he could (Gelbs, LWMC, 313). O'Neill was proud of and interested in his Irish heritage. The plays of the Abbey Players drew on Irish folklore and pagan beliefs, which were associated with the peasant class. Their plays presented the types of earthy characters O'Neill was interested in, and the realistic style was refreshing compared to the melodramatic style he had been raised with. In an interview with Charles A. Merrill of the *Boston Sunday Globe* in 1923 O'Neill said:

> My early experience with the theatre through my father really made me revolt against it. As a boy I saw so much of the old, ranting, artificial, romantic stage stuff that I always had a sort of contempt for the theatre.
>
> It was seeing the Irish Players for the first time that gave me a glimpse of my opportunity. The first year that they came over here I went to see everything they did. I thought then and I still think that they demonstrated the possibilities of naturalistic acting better than any other company (Estrin, 39–40).

During this period, O'Neill received word from his wife, Kathleen Jenkins, that she wanted a divorce. She did not ask for alimony or child support, but she wanted evidence of adultery, the only grounds for divorce in New York State at the time. A friend of the Jenkins's, a lawyer named James C.

Kathleen Jenkins, O'Neill's first wife, and Eugene O'Neill Jr., ca. 1912 (Sheaffer-O'Neill Collection, Connecticut College)

Warren, made the arrangements. On 29 December 1911, O'Neill went out to dinner with Warren and others. After making the rounds of the bars, the group ended up at a brothel near Times Square. There, as Warren testified later, he found O'Neill in bed with a woman in an adulterous situation (Sheaffer, SP, 206). The divorce became final the following July.

Even though he had agreed to the set-up, apparently O'Neill found the whole adultery entrapment scenario greatly demeaning. He fell into a deep depression and in early January attempted suicide. James O'Neill's press secretary, Jimmy Blyth, had become friends with the younger O'Neill and frequented Jimmy's. He became concerned when O'Neill did not wake up one morning. Blyth forced his way into O'Neill's room at Jimmy's and found him passed out after having taken the barbiturate Veronal. Sheaffer was told that Blyth and other lodgers worked in pairs for hours keeping O'Neill on his feet to work off the effects of the barbiturate. Every so often, after a few trips around the block, the men would escape the January cold by ducking back into Jimmy's for warming shots of whiskey (Sheaffer, SP, 209).[36]

Like his exposure to the Abbey Players, O'Neill's survival seems to have been a turning point. Once again he had hit rock bottom and pulled himself out of it. O'Neill would reflect on this experience in *Strange Interlude* when Darrell, referring to Nina, says "she's piled on too many destructive experiences. A few more and she'll dive for the gutter just to get the security that comes from knowing she's touched bottom and there's no further to go!" (O'Neill CP2, 663). Not long after the suicide attempt O'Neill decided to leave New York and his life among sailors and join his father's tour of *The Count of Monte Cristo*.

But Jimmy the Priest's remained a touchstone for O'Neill. He returned whenever he was in New York to catch up with old friends. At Jimmy's he had almost ended his life, but his seafaring friends had helped him to pull himself from the depths. Years later he told his second wife, Agnes Boulton, that he had to write a play about Jimmy the Priest's. He said, "Oh, God, those old days! Nobody'd believe it, nobody'd understand it" (Boulton, 204). Carlotta Monterey, O'Neill's third wife, said that she and her husband had lived in, and traveled to, some of the most beautiful places in the world, but that all this was less important to him than his time "on the beach" in Buenos Aires or at Jimmy the Priest's: "drank too

The American Line SS *St. Louis* on which O'Neill's friend Driscoll sailed
(Mystic Seaport, Rosenfeld Collection 1984.187.B381)

much and inferior liquor, and wore his body and soul out, without proper food or even a bed at night" (Sheaffer, SP, 191).

On one of his trips to Fulton Street, in 1915, O'Neill learned that Driscoll, his stoker friend from the American Line, had killed himself a few months earlier (Sheaffer, SP, 335). Driscoll had been serving as a lead fireman on the SS *St. Louis*. The captain reported that he jumped overboard at sea. He was picked up by one of the ship's boats, but he was dead by the time he was brought aboard. He was 37 at the time.[37] Driscoll was one of the last people O'Neill would have expected to commit suicide— he had seen Driscoll as so strong and confident. When Mary Mullett asked O'Neill why Driscoll had committed suicide, O'Neill responded: "That's what I asked myself. 'Why?' It was the why of Driscoll's suicide that gave me the germ of the idea for my play, *The Hairy Ape*" (Estrin, 31).

Jimmy the Priest's finally fell victim to Prohibition. In December of 1919 O'Neill read in the newspaper that James "Jimmy the Priest" Condon and his bartender had been arrested for homicide. Several of their lodgers and other patrons had died from poisoned liquor. It was believed that Jimmy had refused to deal with a particular bootlegger and in retribution the bootlegger tainted the liquor. The prosecution fell apart in court because all the victims had also been drinking in other establishments the day they died. Although he avoided conviction, Jimmy the Priest was ruined and closed his venerable watering hole the day after the trial (Black, 239–40). But by then Eugene O'Neill was well along his course in a different direction.

O'Neill (left) with two friends along the Thames River in New London, ca. 1913
(Sheaffer–O'Neill Collection, Connecticut College)

The Return to New London

"If this isn't the deadest burg I ever struck!

Bet they take the sidewalks in after nine o'clock!"

—Belle, *Ah, Wilderness!*

In the years 1912 and 1913, O'Neill gave up his vagabond life to become a writer. After his suicide attempt in New York in January of 1912, O'Neill joined the family on his father's vaudeville tour of a shortened version of *The Count of Monte Cristo*. They returned to New York in March, and by April they were in New London for the summer. The O'Neills installed a furnace and winterized the Monte Cristo Cottage that year. In July, O'Neill's divorce from Kathleen became final. There is no conclusive evidence that he had yet seen his son.

In August, O'Neill began to work for the *New London Telegraph* as a reporter, a job arranged by his father with the editor, Frederick P. Latimer. O'Neill covered everything from barroom brawls to elegant weddings. He later referred to himself as a "bum" reporter who was true to his training at Betts Academy but poor at pursuing the journalist's search for facts. In reporting on the knifing of a woman by a man on Bradley Street, he described the scene in great detail but neglected to mention who the individuals were and what relationship brought them to blows. Latimer chastised O'Neill for being too descriptive and not getting facts and details. He acknowledged that O'Neill's stories were creative, but encouraged him to remember the important details of who, what, when, where, and why that comprise accurate reporting.

O'Neill wrote a *Telegraph* article about a schooner that was driven onto the rocks off Fishers Island. After giving the correct name of the schooner, *Maggie Ellen,* the writer referred to it as the *"Mary Ellen,"* O'Neill's mother's given name. A few years later O'Neill wrote the one-act play *Where the Cross Is Made* about a crazy captain whose hopes rely on the return of his schooner, the *"Mary Allen,"* which will never return because it has long since been lost (Sheaffer, SP, 230).

O'Neill also wrote poetry for the newspaper's "Laconics" column. "The Call" was published on 19 November 1912 and recounts his time aboard the *Charles Racine:*

> I have eaten my share of "stock fish"
>   On a steel Norwegian bark;
> With hands gripped hard to the royal yard
>   I have swung through the rain and the dark.
> I have hauled upon the braces
>   And bawled the chantey song,
> And the clutch of the wheel had a friendly feel,
>   And the Trade Wind's kiss was strong. . . .
>
> For it's grand to lie on the hatches
>   In the glowing tropic night
> When the sky is clear and the stars seem near
>   And the wake is a trail of light,
> And the old hulk rolls so softly
>   On the swell of the southern sea
> And the engines croon in a drowsy tune
>   And the world is mystery!
> So it's back to the sea, my brother,
>   Back again to the sea. . . . (Sheaffer, SP, 239)

O'Neill respected Latimer and asked the editor to read many of his short stories, poems, and early plays. Latimer told James O'Neill that he was impressed with his son, believing Eugene "did not have merely talent, but a very high order of genius" (Sheaffer, SP, 229). O'Neill once remarked that Latimer was the first person "who really thought I had something to say, and believed I could say it" (Sheaffer, SP, 228).

In the summer of 1912, O'Neill fell in love with Maibelle Scott. Maibelle told the Gelbs that her relationship with O'Neill lasted until 1914. Maibelle's grandfather Thomas Albertson Scott was a prominent figure in O'Neill's neighborhood. Originally from New Jersey, Scott relocated to New London when he was hired to help build Race Rock Lighthouse. He had gone to sea as a young man and, in 1855, at the age of 25, became a captain and part-owner of a vessel. He became a master diver salvaging lost cargoes and ships. It was his skill as a diver that brought him to New London for the construction of Race Rock Lighthouse on a wave-swept ledge at the western tip of Fishers Island, a few miles south of New London. Attempts had been made to mark the ledge to warn ships, but storms and ice floes carried the markers away. Many experts at the time thought the construction of a lighthouse at the site was impossible. Francis Hopkinson Smith, who had built the foundation for the Statue of Liberty, was hired as engineer of the project. Scott, who had done the difficult submarine work for the Brooklyn Bridge in 1869, was construction foreman. The work began in 1871, and the lighthouse was finally completed in 1878. Smith wrote a fictionalized account of Scott's building of the lighthouse in his book, *Caleb West, Master Diver,* which was published in 1898 and became a best-seller. Upon completion of the lighthouse, Scott stayed on in New London and established a marine salvage business not far from the O'Neills' home on Pequot Avenue. Scott incorporated the business with his son Thomas A. Scott Jr. in 1903 as T. A. Scott Company, Inc. The elder Scott died in 1907, but the business prospered under the son.

In late November of 1912 O'Neill was diagnosed with tuberculosis (TB), and in December his father arranged for him to enter the Fairfield County State Sanatorium in Shelton, Connecticut, where some well-to-do New Londoners were patients at the time. In the autobiographical *Long Day's Journey into Night*—which is set in August 1912—Edmund's accusation that his father sent him to a cheap state institution may be interpreted as unfair. The reality is that it had a good reputation.

O'Neill received a favorable prognosis that he had a good chance of a full recovery with proper rest, food, and treatment. But within two days he checked himself out and went to New York City to see his father. James and Eugene argued over the sanatorium, which resulted in James sending O'Neill to two nationally known TB specialists and making arrangements for O'Neill to be admitted to an excellent private institution, Gaylord Farm Sanatorium in Wallingford, Connecticut. O'Neill was admitted on Christmas Eve 1912 (Black, 130–32).

Under the guidance of Dr. David R. Lyman, cold fresh air, a good diet, and some exercise were the mainstays for treatment at Gaylord. As his health improved, O'Neill also matured intellectually during his stay. "It was at Gaylord that my mind got the chance to establish itself, to digest and evaluate the impressions of many past years in which one experience had crowded on another with never a second's reflection," he commented later (Sheaffer, SP, 252).

O'Neill's stay at Gaylord lasted just over five months. What might have been a setback instead can be credited for starting him on the path to becoming a playwright. Though unaccustomed to the imposed inactivity, O'Neill benefited greatly from the time to reflect on the past and the future. About a year after leaving Gaylord, O'Neill wrote to Dr. Lyman expressing interest in returning for a visit: "If, as they say, it is sweet to visit the place one was born in, then it will be doubly sweet for me to visit the place I was reborn in—for the second birth was the only one which had my full approval."[38]

Dr. Lyman advised O'Neill to get plenty of sunshine and fresh air and avoid the alcohol and high living to which he had been accustomed back in New London. James O'Neill acted on that advice by buying his son a used 18-foot Atlantic dory. The boat cost $200, and the entire stay at Gaylord cost James O'Neill $167.36 (Sheaffer, SP, 258). According to Sheaffer, O'Neill spent many hours on the Thames River stretched naked in the bottom of the boat. Passengers on the Block Island ferry complained because the dory sometimes drifted into the view of the steamer. The complaints did not deter O'Neill from sunbathing.

In the late summer of 1913, James O'Neill was preparing to go on tour in *Joseph and his Brethren*. Ella and Jamie were to accompany him. In light of the doctor's advice, it did not seem prudent for Eugene to accompany them. While his family was on tour O'Neill boarded with the Rippin family, who ran a boardinghouse called the Packard across Pequot Avenue, not far from the Monte Cristo Cottage. The O'Neills were in the habit of having their meals at the Packard when they were in New London.

O'Neill had his own room upstairs, but he liked to sleep on the back porch at night, as the patients did at Gaylord. The water was only a few feet away, and he would be lulled to sleep as if he were at sea. The Rippin daughters, Emily and Jessica, told Sheaffer that O'Neill developed the routine of writing every morning, then taking a long swim, writing in the afternoon, taking a long walk or rowing in his boat with Maibelle

O'Neill after a swim in the Thames River on 1 January, 1914. O'Neill sent the photograph to Dr. Lyman at Gaylord Sanatorium as proof that he was following the doctor's advice for exercise and fresh air (Sheaffer–O'Neill Collection, Connecticut College)

Scott or another girl, and sometimes continuing to write in the evening. This writing routine stayed with him most of his life.

Jessica Rippin introduced O'Neill to Clayton Hamilton, a book-review editor for *Vogue* and *Bookman,* a lecturer on drama at Columbia University, and an emerging drama critic. Hamilton stayed with the Rippins on occasion, and O'Neill asked Hamilton for advice on a play. "Never mind how plays are written," Hamilton responded. "Write down what you know about the sea, and about men who sail before the mast. This has been done in the novel; it has been done in the short-story; it has not been done in the drama. Keep your eye on life—on life as you have seen it; and to hell with the rest" (Bowen, 60).

While at the Rippins', O'Neill wrote a number of plays, including *Children of the Sea,* which with some minor revisions later became *Bound East for Cardiff.* In 1919 O'Neill wrote to Jessica Rippin, noting that he had never worked harder than during that winter when he lived in their home. He also expressed his gratitude to the family and particularly Mrs. Rippin for giving him a "real touch of a home life," something he had not experienced as an actor's son (Bogard, 85).

Jessica Rippin told the Gelbs that O'Neill once said to her: "My wife and I will live on a barge. I'll live at one end and she'll live at the other, and we'll never see each other except when the urge strikes us" (Gelbs, 246). O'Neill treasured his solitude and at the same time liked the idea of having a wife who would care for him. His thoughts about life on a barge probably reflected his perception that the solitude of Chris Christopherson's life was idyllic.

In early May of 1914 O'Neill ended his stay at the Rippins' and prepared the Monte Cristo Cottage for the arrival of his family. They were returning earlier than expected. O'Neill confided in Mrs. Rippin that his mother had been ill, had spent time in a sanatorium, and was now better. Over the years, Ella O'Neill had tried a number of things to end her addiction to morphine; this time it was finally successful.

That August, Gorham Press of Boston published O'Neill's *Thirst and Other One Act Plays,* which included *The Web, Warnings, Fog,* and *Recklessness.* James O'Neill financed the book. Clayton Hamilton's favorable reviews of the book appeared in *Bookman* and *The Nation* almost a year after it was released.

Boats moored in Thames River along Pequot Avenue, not far from the Monte Cristo Cottage (Sheaffer–O'Neill Collection, Connecticut College)

Hamilton had encouraged O'Neill to take George Pierce Baker's playwriting course at Harvard University, and he enrolled in the fall. In the course he learned to write a detailed scenario of a play before the dialogue, a technique he used throughout his career.

During the course, O'Neill wrote *The Second Engineer*, which he later renamed *The Personal Equation*. Unhappy with the work he created during Baker's course, O'Neill destroyed his copies of *The Personal Equation*, but a copy was found years later in the Harvard Library. Sheaffer asserts that the play is more autobiographical than one would think. O'Neill uses himself as the inspiration for the pivotal character, Tom, a rebellious youth. But the more interesting character is the young man's father, an engineer who is devoted to his steam engines rather than his son, as James O'Neill was devoted to *The Count of Monte Cristo* and forsook his family (Sheaffer, SP, 307). James kept his children at a distance and devoted his attention to his stage career. On one level he begrudgingly

gave his sons money, but on another level he was very supportive. James and the engineer in *The Personal Equation* are obsessed with the vehicle of their careers, a play for the former and an engine for the latter. What had originally been a job and a means of financial stability became an obsession and shut the men off from an emotional connection with their sons. In *The Personal Equation* O'Neill explored some of the themes that he would later address in *The Hairy Ape,* particularly the devotion that the engineer and Yank share for powerful steam engines.

After his year at Harvard, O'Neill returned to New London for the summer, at a time when his father was becoming increasingly concerned about finances because his producers had filed for bankruptcy. So O'Neill decided not to return to Harvard in the fall for the second year of Baker's course and instead went to New York. Through his friend Louis Holladay, he met Terry Carlin, an anarchist well-respected by the Greenwich Village radicals. Carlin was 60 and O'Neill had just turned 27. During that fall and winter they lived together in an abandoned building in Manhattan (Black, 186). Occasionally, O'Neill would wander downtown and visit his old friends at Jimmy the Priest's. During one of these visits he learned that his old American Line friend Driscoll had committed suicide (Sheaffer, 335).

As the summer of 1916 approached, O'Neill was eager to leave New York City, but he did not want to spend another summer with his family in New London. Carlin suggested that O'Neill accompany him to Provincetown, Massachusetts. Carlin had spent summers there before, and O'Neill had heard of it from other friends in Greenwich Village. By late June, O'Neill and Carlin were on their way to Provincetown.

O'Neill at Doc Ganey's cottage along the Niantic River in East Lyme, Connecticut, ca. 1913 (Sheaffer-O'Neill Collection, Connecticut College)

Provincetown harbor and town hall, ca. 1900 (Mystic Seaport 1979.175.1)

Maritime Provincetown

**"Provincetown—a fishing village at the end of Cape Cod,
hard to get to and get out of, but a grand place to be alone
and undisturbed when you want to work."**

—Eugene O'Neill, in a letter to Jessica Rippin (Bogard, 85)

Although it is located on a sand spit at the very tip of Cape Cod,
Provincetown bears many similarities to more substantial New London
in its rich maritime history and generations of dependence on the sea for
a livelihood. Because of Provincetown's large and relatively sheltered harbor it became the primary fishing port on Cape Cod and held onto that
capacity long after many of the other, smaller Cape harbors silted in.
Mary Heaton Vorse chronicled Provincetown in her 1942 book *Time and
the Town*. "It lives and breathes through the harbor," she noted. "The lively comings and goings of the vessels are the very core of the town's life"
(Vorse, 147–48). In addition to fishing, like New London, Provincetown
had a history of whaling, trade with the West Indies, and associated maritime industries. Activity in the harbor increased during inclement weather
as vessels en route to and from Boston sought shelter during storms.

Cape Cod's maritime heyday lasted from the 1830s until after the
Civil War, with Provincetown reaching its peak in the 1880s. Provincetown whalers went to Arctic and Antarctic waters after whales and sea
elephants, and Provincetown fishing schooners sailed as far as the Grand
Banks of Newfoundland after mackerel and codfish. Provincetown continued building wharves to support the various industries and, though
small, it became the richest town per capita in the state of Massachusetts.
The Old Colony Railroad reached the town in 1873, operating two trains
daily in each direction between Provincetown and Boston, with extra
trains added in the summer. The railroad brought Provincetown within
four hours of Boston.

Between the 1850s and 1870s Provincetown had the largest fleet of
fishing and whaling vessels on Cape Cod, with twice the catch of all the

Provincetown looking toward the east end, ca. 1900 (Mystic Seaport 1979.175.3)

other towns combined (Ruckstuhl, v). Though not as prominent a whaling port as New London, Provincetown was home port to a total of 120 whaling vessels from the 1820s to 1920.

Whaling was the impetus for Portuguese immigration. As it became more difficult for whaling captains to hire crews in New England, they began to stop in the Azores and Cape Verde Islands to recruit crew. The crew generally returned to the ship's home port, and once in Provincetown many of the Portuguese stayed on to work in the town's maritime trades.

Cod fishing was one of the most important industries to the town, with fertile fishing grounds on the raised portions of the continental shelf called banks, extending from Georges Bank off Cape Cod to the Grand Banks of Newfoundland. As with whaling, the ownership of a fishing vessel and the voyage was treated like a company, with shares being divided into sixteenths. The community was involved. When a new vessel was built the outfitters took an eighth, the captain had an eighth, the sailmaker, blockmaker, sparmaker, and rigger had a sixteenth, and other members of the community took the remaining shares (Smith, 60).

In the third quarter of the nineteenth century, Provincetown fishing schooners were away from home for two to three months at a time, using salt to preserve their catch. The fishermen used hooks and lines—either handlines that could be dangled from the vessel's rail or used away from the vessel in a small boat called a dory; or longline trawls with hundreds of hooks that lay on the bottom and were set and hauled by the fishermen in dories. The fish were split on deck and then the catch was salted and stored in the hold. Once the hold was full the schooner returned home. The catch was off-loaded and the salted cod was washed, resalted, and laid out on racks called fish flakes to air-dry for market. Most Provincetown wharves, and even private yards, were lined with fish flakes.

By the mid-1880s fresh fishing had superseded salt fishing, and in 1885 the Provincetown fresh fish industry was worth nearly a million dollars. Many of the other Cape Cod towns, such as Truro and Wellfleet, had

Provincetown looking toward the west end, ca. 1900 (Mystic Seaport 1979.175.2)

already stopped fishing by then. To supply the fleet, other fishermen set trap or weir nets near Provincetown to snare bait and food fish. Several companies built cold-storage plants in Provincetown for the fish and increased the number of weirs for bait for the fishing fleet (Vorse, 70–71). In the process, some of the old, small fishing wharves were abandoned.

The new business of fresh fishing required that vessels get their catch to market faster. Generally the first schooner to arrive in port received the highest price for its fish. More than ever before, fishing schooners were built for speed. And their destination changed from the Grand Banks to nearby Georges Bank. Inspired to hyperbole, Mary Heaton Vorse wrote about the beauty of the "great fresh fishermen," the speed of the schooners, and the great pride of the crews:

> if you looked out of the window at sunrise or just before, you would see a sight of glory. The one-hundred-twenty-five-foot schooners would be getting underway. . . . One after another would make sail until as many as twenty-five of these beauties rounded the point. . . .
>
> The race of these rival skippers for market has probably outfooted any of the formal fisherman's races, though we have no record of them. In those days when fish were scarce and the man who made market first got the high prices, if he came in after stormy weather with halibut he might make a fortune for himself and his crew. The racing of two of these great boats was one of the romances of the sea, the winner coming in with a broom tied to his mast, indicating he had swept all before him.
>
> The great captains strode the streets of Provincetown with the security of great rulers. Here was the moral equivalent of war. Here were danger and adventure. Here was a gamble so great that it included risking one's living and one's life. The men who sailed under these great captains were as proud of their vessels as if they owned her themselves (Vorse, 167–69).

In the shift to fresh fishing, the "great captains" and their crews became largely of Portuguese extraction, bringing a colorful ethnic feel to the waterfront and streets of Provincetown.

There were many dangers associated with fishing on Georges Bank, located just about 100 miles east of Cape Cod. The area is prone to thick fogs, sudden storms, and strong currents across its shoals. All of the banks were on or near the transatlantic shipping lanes, and it was not uncommon for an anchored fishing schooner, or its dories, to be run down by a steamer in a fog. The schooner *"We're Here"* in Rudyard Kipling's *Captains Courageous* nearly suffered such a fate. Mary Heaton Vorse recounted a story she heard in one of the fish houses of Provincetown. Louis "Tindrawers" and his dorymate, Lopez, were separated from their schooner in a fog. When the fog lifted, they could not see their vessel. They rowed for two days and two nights and ended up on the "back side" of Provincetown, thinking they had been unlucky being separated from their schooner, only to learn that a steamer had run her down with the loss of all on board. They were the only survivors (Vorse, 165).

It was also possible for a schooner's anchor cable to part in a storm, and for the suddenly free vessel to go careening into other schooners at anchor. At least 15 New England fishing schooners—and 120 men—were lost at anchor on Georges Bank during a single gale in February 1862.

O'Neill would have known of these dangers. He had read *Captains Courageous* in his youth, and his experiences with the American Line showed him the locales and conditions firsthand. His early one-act play, *Fog,* is certainly influenced by that knowledge.

Until the Cape Cod Canal opened in July of 1914, all coastal shipping to and from Boston and ports further northeast had to travel around Cape Cod. When storms came in, the northeasterly winds put the treacherous "back side" of Cape Cod on their lee, and many ships stranded on the shoals along the shore. Even with the opening of the canal, many vessels still had to take the outside route. Initially the canal was not deep enough to accommodate large vessels or heavily laden barges.

Because of the numerous shipwrecks on Cape Cod and other exposed shores of the United States, Congress established the U.S. Life-Saving Service, which was formed in 1871, becoming an independent entity in 1878, and merging with the U.S. Revenue Cutter Service in 1915 to become the U.S. Coast Guard. (The Lighthouse Service, established earlier, was brought under the Coast Guard in 1939.) With its many skilled boatmen and fishermen, Provincetown was a recruiting ground for the Life-Saving Service. "The history of the coast guard is the core of Provincetown's history," wrote Mary Heaton Vorse. "For Provincetown's

**Top: The waterfront in the east end of Provincetown, ca. 1910
(Sheaffer-O'Neill Collection, Connecticut College)**

Bottom: A shipyard along Commercial Street in Provincetown, ca. 1910 (Sheaffer–O'Neill Collection, Connecticut College)

history is the story of men against the sea. Dates by which this town reckons time are those of great storms. Here stories are not of battles, but of the long-sustained fight for safety at sea" (Vorse, 62).

Along the nation's busiest and most exposed coasts, such as Cape Cod, the U.S. Life-Saving Service established surfboat stations for rescues. By 1902 Cape Cod had 13 stations located along the outer shore an average of six miles apart. Provincetown had four stations: Wood End, Race Point, Peaked Hill Bars, and High Head. A captain manned each station year-round, and seven other men joined him for the more severe weather months, August through May. The surfmen of the station crew were responsible for keeping a lookout for vessels in distress or in danger of being forced ashore. During daylight hours they stood watch from a lookout on the top of the station, but during periods of limited visibility and at night they patrolled the beaches. On these patrols, one man set out in each direction and met the man from the neighboring station. They exchanged tokens as proof that they had completed their patrol and then returned to their station. If the surfman spotted a vessel approaching danger or already in distress they would set off a flare to inform the vessel that it had been seen and alert the rest of the crew at the station.

The U.S. Life-Saving Service recorded 540 wrecks on Cape Cod between 1880 and 1903 (Ruckstuhl, 75). One of the most dangerous stretches of that treacherous coast is Peaked Hill Bars. Just offshore, two sand bars run parallel to the shore for about six miles. The bars are always shifting and the depths vary (Dalton, 73).

In the event of a wreck, the crew would often drag their surfboat on a cart down the beach and launch it into the breaking sea to rescue those on the stranded vessel, landing them through the surf. If the surf broke too heavily, they would rely on the breeches buoy apparatus. In this case, a beach cart trundled a small cannon called a Lyle gun and long lengths of rope to a spot near the wreck. The Lyle gun fired a light line across the stranded vessel, which her crew used to haul aboard a pulley with a long rope running through it. Once that was secured on board, the lifesavers were able to pull things to and from the vessel. The first thing to go out to the vessel was a heavy hawser. When that was made fast on board, the lifesavers sent out the breeches buoy—a life preserver with canvas "pants"—like a trolley to bring the crew ashore. Each week, the surfmen practiced their skills.

The Peaked Hill Bars Life-Saving Station before it was converted into a private residence (Pilgrim Monument and Provincetown Museum)

The schooner barges *Tuckahoe* and *Rutherford*, washed up on the beach at Peaked Hill Bars, 1915 (Pilgrim Monument and Provincetown Museum)

In J.W. Dalton's chronicle of the U.S. Life-Saving Service, *The Life Savers of Cape Cod,* published in 1902, is an account of the wreck of the sloop *C.E. Trumbull,* which ran aground on Peaked Hill Bars on a night in November 1880. During the rescue of the *Trumbull's* crew, the Peaked Hill crew launched their surfboat with Captain David H. Atkins in command and Surfmen Charles P. Kelley, Frank A. Mayo, Elisha Taylor, Samuel Fisher, and Isaiah Young at the oars. They rescued three crewmen from the sloop and brought them back to shore, then returned to the sloop to get the two remaining men. As the surfboat was alongside and getting ready to receive the men, the sloop's boom swung around and caught the surfboat, capsizing it. All the men were thrown into the churning and frigid sea. Captain Atkins was lost in the dark immediately, two of the men died as they tried to get back into the surfboat, and three reached the shore after a long struggle in the surf. The members of the crew that had remained on shore pulled Kelley, Fisher, and Young out of the surf. The three were suffering from hypothermia and near death. The bodies of Atkins, Mayo, and Taylor were found on the beach by the crew of a

The waterfront in the east end of Provincetown, ca. 1910 (Sheaffer-O'Neill Collection, Connecticut College)

neighboring station. The loss of so many men and in a single accident was devastating to the community. Their memory was honored for years thereafter.

The Life-Saving Service—later the Coast Guard—was not the only federal service in Provincetown. Provincetown had three lighthouses—Race Point, Long Point at the entrance to the harbor, and Wood End between them. A few miles away on the high bluff of the Highlands was Cape Cod or Highland Light, one of the brightest lights on the coast, which could be seen nearly 20 miles at sea. These lights were tended by a keeper, who usually lived at the site, often with his family.

The U.S. Navy's Atlantic Squadron conducted summer exercises near Provincetown and anchored in the harbor from the late 1870s to the start of World War I. Everett Ladd Clarke wrote in *New England Magazine:* "The spectacle is always an interesting one. The great ships swinging at anchor or going and coming on their mysterious errands, in response to the unending signals, brilliant at night or sharply outlined against the blue waters by day, hold the attention tirelessly for hours" (Ruckstuhl, 68).

By the early twentieth century Provincetown had begun to evolve into an artists' colony. In 1899 Charles W. Hawthorne established the Cape Cod School of Art in Provincetown, which was soon followed by the schools of George Elmer Brown and E. Ambrose Webster. The schools provided the nucleus for the art colony and had an important impact on young artists. Provincetown was a hospitable place for artists, with inexpensive housing and studio space available. Many of the sail lofts, fish houses, and other maritime structures were taken over and turned into studios. It had great appeal because it was remote, but there was easy access from Boston and New York, with a direct connection from Greenwich Village. The Fall River Line steamboats left from lower Manhattan and terminated in Fall River, Massachusetts, where there was a connecting train to Provincetown (Egan, 31).

Hildegarde Hawthorne's 1916 book about New England seaport towns had this to say: "Provincetown more than any other of the seaports we had seen, gives a sense of unchangedness. . . . There it lies among its wild sand-hills beside its wonderful harbour, quaint, lovable, unique, full of stories of the sea as it is of sea wind, murmuring like a shell and restful beyond words." Her sister and traveling companion joined in: "It seems to have learned the lesson of immortality from the sea and the sand. It will endure as they endure, with immaterial changes and telling constancy. I want to put on a purple smock and rent a studio on an old wharf and stay here forever, don't you?" Her sister responded, "I do" (Hawthorne, 237).

The Provincetown O'Neill came to in 1916 was a community with a rich seafaring heritage trying to redefine itself after the decline of its maritime industries. It is more remote than New London, almost completed surrounded by water with the feel of an island. Agnes Edwards noted: "It is here that we find the quintessence of the seafaring atmosphere, for although the inhabitants no longer depend exclusively upon the ocean to bring them their means of livelihood, yet in a place so completely surrounded by water, peculiar and charming customs become an integral part of the daily life. . . . The atmosphere, both actual and figuratively, is soaked with salt water and the nameless and numberless associations which are part of it" (Edwards, 164–65).

Mary Heaton Vorse voiced her thoughts: "Provincetown men are not landsmen. Almost without exception they have at one time or anoth-

Mary Heaton Vorse with friends in Provincetown (front row) Neith Boyce, Beatrix Hapgood, Vorse, Hippolyte Havel, (second row) Harry Weinberger, Hutchins Hapgood, and Miriam Hapgood, ca. 1916 (Sheaffer–O'Neill Collection, Connecticut College)

er 'followed the sea.' Certainly their forebears have. Provincetowners have spent so much of their time on the sea in ships that they look upon houses as a sort of land ship or a species of houseboat and therefore not subject to the laws of houses" (Vorse, 89). This was an ideal atmosphere for O'Neill, embracing so much of what he felt for the sea. An additional positive feature was that Provincetown was a dry town, enabling O'Neill to stick to his writing. It stayed dry until Prohibition was repealed in 1933.

Theater on the wharf in Provincetown, where O'Neill's plays were first produced (Sheaffer–O'Neill Collection, Connecticut College)

Arrival in Provincetown

"I filled in Provincetown as my residence. As I was married there under that understanding, and as I have lived there the greater part of the last three years, I think I may justly regard it as my home town—(if I ever had any!)."
—Eugene O'Neill to John Francis, 8 March 1919 (Sheaffer-O'Neill Collection)

In the spring of 1916 O'Neill realized he needed to get away from the distractions of New York City if he wanted to return to his writing. Some of his Greenwich Village artist and writer friends were going to Provincetown for the summer and he decided to go along. According to Sheaffer, O'Neill heard from his friends that Provincetown was as close as he could get to the sea, and that a group there put on one-act plays. O'Neill was still living off an allowance from his father, who probably supported his son's departure from the diversions of New York.

O'Neill and his friend Terry Carlin—drifter, roomate, and drinking companion—decided to go for the summer. O'Neill has been described as stepping off the steamer from Boston at the Railroad Wharf in Provincetown dressed as a sailor and carrying a rucksack. O'Neill and Carlin rented a flat over John Francis's store, which had a view of the bay. Francis was a local businessman, who in addition to his store dealt in real estate, insurance, and additional ventures that supported the summer residents. Others of the Greenwich Village crowd lived in flats owned by Francis, including John Reed and Louise Bryant. Reed began writing for the Socialist newspaper *The Masses* in 1913 and later became friends with Vladimir Lenin, witnessed the Bolshevik Revolution in Russia, and recorded the events in his best-known work, *Ten Days that Shook the World,* published in 1919. After publication of the book he became the leader of the U.S. Communist Labor Party, was indicted for treason, and escaped to the Soviet Union, where he died in 1920. Louise Bryant was married to a dentist in Portland, Oregon, but the couple's marriage was liberal for the time. She maintained her maiden name, and her husband rarely intruded on her

O'Neill and John Reed in Provincetown, ca. 1916 (Sheaffer–O'Neill Collection, Connecticut College)

private domain, a rented studio where she wrote and painted. Bryant met John Reed in Portland while he was visiting his mother, and they fell in love. She followed him to New York, and Reed remained devoted to her, even though she had affairs with others, including O'Neill. Bryant also followed Reed to Russia, but she was unwilling to be as public about their shared political views as he was.

Terry Carlin was a friend of Susan Glaspell, one of the organizers of the Provincetown group that put on plays. Glaspell had been a reporter for the Des Moines, Iowa, *News* before dedicating her time to writing short stories, novels, and then plays. When Carlin and Glaspell met on the street in Provincetown, she asked him if he had any plays. He did not, but he told her that his friend O'Neill had some one-act plays with him. This exchange led to the first reading of *Bound East for Cardiff* (then called *Children of the Sea*) at the home of Mary Heaton Vorse, who recalled: "There was no one there during that reading who did not recognize the quality of this play. Here was something new, the true feeling of the sea" (Vorse, 121).

Vorse had come to Provincetown in the summer of 1907 for a week's vacation, but from that point on she made it her home. She was an accomplished writer—a pioneer of labor journalism and soon to be a war correspondent—covering the Lawrence textile strike in 1912 and later the aftermath of World War I from Europe. She also wrote short stories, which she referred to as "lollypops," for popular magazines.

During that summer of 1916 the Provincetown group offered *Bound East for Cardiff*—O'Neill's first play to be produced—as its season-opening production. Later that summer the group also produced O'Neill's one-act play *Thirst*. The group presented 12 plays that summer, including works by John Reed, Louise Bryant, and Susan Glaspell. The group had come together the year before to establish a new American theater, one free of the "hackneyed melodramas and frothy comedies on Broadway" (Egan, 4–5). But it was the production of *Bound East for Cardiff*, with its realism and the depiction of the working class, that helped the Provincetown group realize its dream of instilling new life into the American theater.

The Provincetown group presented their plays at the Wharf Theater, which was an old fish house on a wharf owned by Mary Heaton Vorse. Members of the group directed and acted in each other's plays. The artistic and intellectual community that summered in Provincetown was the perfect audience for the emerging theater company.

By the end of the summer the group had gained momentum in its quest to present plays and playwrights that broke away from the traditional fare being presented in New York. The Provincetown group perceived that the New York theater was at a low point and that playwriting had become a trade and not an art. There were a number of playwrights at the time who wrote well-constructed dramas, but they had become formulaic. O'Neill's plays were the first to venture into the new genre of realism and tragedy that had been developed by European playwrights Henrik Ibsen, Anton Chekov, George Bernard Shaw, and August Strindberg. Little of their work had been seen in the United States by this time, but thanks to "Doc" Ganey, O'Neill had read some of their plays in New London, and the Abbey Players had expanded his perspective on theatrical realism. The Provincetown group felt that they had discovered something new that they wanted to carry back to New York.

In early September, before returning to New York, the Provincetown group decided to call themselves the Provincetown Players, and at O'Neill's suggestion they named their new home in New York the

Playwright's Theater. At its founding there were 29 members, including John Reed, George Cram Cooke, Max Eastman, Frederick Burt, O'Neill, Louise Bryant, Susan Glaspell, Mary Heaton Vorse, and Marguerite and William Zorach (Deutsch, 16–17).

The Provincetown Players were not the only artists revolting against the staid art of the previous generation. A parallel movement existed among painters, particularly George Bellows—with whom O'Neill had shared a farmhouse in Zion, New Jersey—and John Sloan, both of the Ashcan School. Bellows and Sloan were encouraged to take to the streets of New York and document urban life. Their paintings captured immigrants, dockworkers, prostitutes, and the crowded conditions of city life. The painters treated their subjects with a sympathetic eye in the same way that O'Neill perceived his characters.

During their first season in New York, the Provincetown Players produced eight different bills of one-act plays between November and March, a total of 24 plays. They renovated a building on Macdougal Street in Greenwich Village for their theater. Four of O'Neill's plays were

Men of the Docks by George Bellows (1912). (First purchase of the Randolph-Macon Art Association, 1920, courtesy Maier Museum of Art, Randolph-Macon Woman's College, Lynchburg, Virginia)

The Atlantic House in Provincetown, where O'Neill wrote *In the Zone, Ile, The Long Voyage Home,* and *The Moon of the Caribbees* (Pilgrim Monument and Provincetown Museum)

staged during that first New York season, including *Bound East for Cardiff, Before Breakfast, Fog,* and *The Sniper.* It was a successful premier season, both programmatically and financially. No one was paid for their work, except the president and secretary, or received royalties. The actors provided their own costumes, and they borrowed stage props (Deutsch, 21).

In New York the plays gained audiences, but Provincetown was the creative source for the work, and it was where O'Neill did his writing. Other artists were drawn to Provincetown, but the flow of O'Neill's creativity and the body of work he turned out indicates the depth of his emotional connections with that environment. Its isolation, its proximity to the sea, and the absence of alcohol was the perfect formula to stimulate the writer in him. By March of 1917, O'Neill was anxious to leave New York and return to Provincetown. Concerned that the bleakness of Provincetown in March would be more than he could bear alone, O'Neill convinced Harold DePolo, a pulp-fiction writer friend from the Village, to go with him. Sheaffer describes DePolo as one who enjoyed living life to the fullest, was high-spirited, and had a quick-wit and fast temper (Sheaffer, SP, 332). The two friends stayed at one of the only hotels in town, the Atlantic House. Just a few weeks after their arrival, the United States entered World War I. Although Provincetown felt vulnerable to attacks from German U-boats, which stalked ships offshore, the two men remained.

O'Neill wrote in his room or took long walks with his typewriter out to the back shore, overlooking the open Atlantic. He completed four one-act plays, *In the Zone, The Long Voyage Home, The Moon of the Caribbees,* and *Ile.* With the exception of *Ile,* the one-acts are about the crew of the fictitious "SS *Glencairn,*" who are the same characters as in *Bound East for Cardiff.* In addition to the plays, he wrote two short stories, "The Hairy Ape," which he later destroyed, and "Tomorrow," published that June in *Seven Arts* magazine.

Ile was inspired by the experiences of Provincetown whaling captain John A. Cook, and his wife Viola. According to one account, Mary Heaton Vorse told O'Neill about the Cooks. O'Neill suggested that Vorse write their story, but she declined because she knew the family too well. O'Neill said that he would use the story for a play (Gelb, LWMC, 613).

Ile tells the story of a whaling captain obsessed with the pursuit of whales. His vessel is trapped in the Arctic ice, forcing him to stay longer than planned. When the ice starts to break up the captain decides, against the pleas of his wife and crew, to pursue whales further north instead of turning for home. The captain resorts to threats and brutality to keep the crew in line, and his wife, feeling isolated and longing for home, goes mad.

Viola Fish Cook was born in Hyannis, Massachusetts, in 1855 and married John Cook of Provincetown at the age of 22. He was two years her junior (Coogan, 121). Mrs. Cook accompanied her husband aboard the bark-rigged steam whaler *Bowhead* on a voyage that began in March of 1903 and lasted 44 months—instead of the 20 months originally planned. Captain Cook had his crew sign an agreement for 36 months in case he had to extend the voyage. When the three years passed and they were still in Arctic waters, the crew became mutinous, and a number of them had to be restrained until they agreed to continue to work. Mrs. Cook suffered profound depression from the extended period in the Arctic and from a longing to return home and see grandchildren, who had been born in her absence. A "prominent physician" in Nome, Alaska, said that Mrs. Cook's condition resulted from being in "cold dark conditions for so long" and prescribed that "the only remedy was that of sunshine and

Captain John A. Cook, the inspiration for Captain Keeney in *Ile* (Pilgrim Monument and Provincetown Museum)

Viola Cook, the inspiration for Mrs. Keeney in *Ile*, dressed for the Arctic (Pilgrim Monument and Provincetown Museum)

civilization" (Cook, 299). Captain Cook did not complete the voyage. He turned the command of the *Bowhead* over to a captain he trusted and accompanied his wife home to Provincetown where Mrs. Cook's condition improved slowly.

The Cooks' adventure lends itself to exaggeration. O'Neill used that privilege as a writer of fiction, and others have echoed *Ile*, portraying Mrs. Cook's condition as more severe than it may have been.

Viola Cook was not as fragile as she has been portrayed. She accompanied her husband on a total of five whaling voyages, the first four to the Arctic. Her original objective of going to sea was to improve her health. The first voyage, aboard the steam bark *Navarch*, lasted almost three years and ended in November 1896, a year later than planned. Mrs. Cook had achieved her objective: "vigor and vitality and enduring health were won." At the outset of the voyage she had weighed 93 pounds, and upon her return she weighed 130 pounds *(Boston Sunday Globe, 1905)*. Mrs. Cook was 41 years old at the end of what had not been a profitable voyage.

The Cook's 18-year-old daughter accompanied her parents on the second voyage, aboard the *Bowhead*. They boarded the *Bowhead* in Norway, where Captain Cook had purchased the vessel and had it out-fitted for whaling. They sailed from Norway in January 1898, through the Suez Canal to Yokohama, Japan, where they picked up Arctic whaling supplies shipped from the United States. Whaling in the Arctic Ocean and wintering over in the ice on the north coast of Alaska, they ended the voyage in San Francisco in November 1899. By March of the following year the Cooks were at sea again, without their daughter, for a voyage that lasted just over 19 months, venturing further north than ever before and settling for the winter in an area that Captain Cook described as "a dreary waste. No settlement near by—only natives that follow whalers for trade" (Cook, 219). Mary Heaton Vorse said of Mrs. Cook during this voyage: "she spent a fifty-eight-day spell of unbroken night in the Arctic, the thermometer fifty-seven below zero" (Vorse, 22).

According to Cook, his wife was the only white woman on record to have wintered so far north and east on the Pacific side of the United States. During this trip she was curious about the igloos where the natives lived. She crawled into the entrance, a tunnel between 20 and 40 feet long, and was confronted by snarling dogs. The family came out to see what the commotion was and escorted Mrs. Cook inside. The Eskimo women were very curious about Mrs. Cook and her clothing, and through the course of the winter they became friendly. Mrs. Cook taught them how to sew cloth, and the Eskimo women taught her how to sew furs and leather. The Eskimo women became more adept at their new skill than Mrs. Cook (Cook, 221). The ship was stuck in the ice for a particularly long period, from October 1900 to almost the end of July 1901 (Cook, 232).

Mrs. Cook's fourth and longest voyage was the fateful one in the Arctic where she reportedly went mad. Originally she had not planned on accompanying her husband, and he set out from Provincetown by train to San Francisco without her. However, she changed her mind and met her husband and the ship at Nome, Alaska. Some speculate that her decision to follow her husband was to appease his anger over her desire to stay at home (Coogan, 125–26). The final winter of this voyage was spent at Herschel Island, on the far northeast coast of Alaska, in the company of at least four other ships.

During a typical winter, Arctic whalers grouped together as they prepared to be frozen in. The freeze would start as early as October, and the thaw did not come until April or May. As many as 15 vessels may have wintered over with the Cooks' ship, positioning themselves in a sheltered harbor and letting the ice form around them. Once the ice had formed, snow was banked up around the ship and a wood and snow structure was built over the vessel. The whalers came prepared with provisions for a certain number of winters, and they would supplement their food by sending out hunting parties for deer and by trading with the Eskimos. They acquired dogs and dogsleds to hunt and trade.

Captains' wives were aboard some of the other vessels, and the couples frequently gathered in the evening for dances and dinner parties. Captain Cook noted that they enjoyed listening to their daughter play the piano when she was with them. On occasion a ship's crew might put on a play. "The *Beluga* was especially fitted for entertainments, having a house fitted for theatrical performances," reported Captain Cook. "We were entertained often by companies whose performers were found among members of the several ships" (Cook, 58). One of the plays presented aboard the *Beluga*, called *Baby Elephant*, had a cast of 20 sailors from various ships (Cook, 60).

During the day, if the weather was not too severe, they entertained themselves outside. Viola Cook enjoyed going sledding or taking dogsled rides with the other captains' wives. In an article that appeared in the *Boston Sunday Globe* on Christmas Eve, 1905, Mrs. Cook was quoted: "Coasting from the hills of Herschel down the long incline leading to the ice-hid waters of the cove is a captivating pastime. What matters it if one's nose or cheeks show white patches denoting frost bite? A snow application followed by brisk rubbing removes the frost and restores circulation. Bundled as we are in furs, we suffer no ill except such face touches and the ride down the white long trail in a keen and bracing air is simply exhilarating" *(Boston Sunday Globe, 1905)*.

Even though they were isolated, the collected ships' companies created a community for themselves. Life was bleak due to the cold and endless nights, but it was not as bleak as one would expect or believe. Mrs. Cook wrote:

> Life in the north is enjoyable, not withstanding the excessive cold and darkness and the long isolation. One would suppose the voyager would need to hug the fire to avoid perishing when I tell you the temperature was as low as 57 below zero, and for weeks never rose above 50, during our winter at Ballie Island.
>
> Dense snowstorms, accompanied with bitter cold, does keep us confined for days at a time on occasions, but with clearing weather we take to the open—one needs to for exercise, you know, and really the round of sports that make for the preservation of health and pleasure is not a limited one.
>
> Sewing helps to dispel the monotony that will manifest itself assertively at times. The glories of the northern lights possess a never-ending charm as viewed from the quiet quarter-deck on a calm evening, with the clear-cut eyes of night studding the dark expanse of heavens and sharp, musket-like reports—the cracking of ocean's icy coverlet—sound out where the snowy surface sheet, looking wan and ghostly, stretches afar into the darkness *(Boston Sunday Globe, 1905)*.

Whatever emotional breakdown she may have suffered in the Arctic, the 1903 voyage was not Mrs. Cook's last with her husband. She accompanied him on the *Viola,* a brigantine named for her, on a two-year voyage to the tropics. She had hoped that her health would improve further by being in the tropics for an extended time. When she returned in July 1912 she decided she did not want to go to sea again (Cook, 338–41). But her husband continued to whale, and the *Viola* was among Provincetown's very last whalers. In 1917—the year O'Neill wrote *Ile*—Cook returned with a cargo that included 1,250 barrels of sperm whale oil and 121 pounds of ambergris, valued at $75,000 (Smith, 71). The voyage was quite profitable at a time when, in general, whaling was marginal at best. Wartime had increased the value of some whale products, especially high-grade sperm whale oil, which was used to lubricate fine machinery. Ambergris is a waxy substance occasionally found in the intestines of sperm whales. Extremely rare and valuable, it was highly prized as a fixative in perfume.

Captain Cook wrote an account of his whaling career in the Arctic, which almost surely is tempered in his favor, but appears to be reliable for basic facts. He does not shy away from his feelings for his wife, his distress over her condition, his firm treatment of the crew, and the court's decision when the crew brought suit against him. But the version of the story Eugene O'Neill received is epitomized in Mary Heaton Vorse's rendering: "Mrs. Cook went down to her cabin and turned her back to the porthole and 'Thar she sot.' She stayed there for nine months, until the vessel was full of oil and turned southward again. When Viola Cook came ashore her mind had been shaken by the loneliness and perhaps by the cruelty of her husband" (Vorse, 22).

Though she may have suggested that the Cooks were too close for her to write about, Mary Heaton Vorse found their story irresistible in her efforts to dramatize the characters of Provincetown. In her 1942 book Vorse described Viola Cook:

> What Mrs. Cook may have seen of brutality, she wouldn't admit into her consciousness. She would be seen in her yard, brushing out the Captain's clothes when he was expected back. She would say to herself, "No better pair of legs went into any pants than Johnny Cook's legs. . . ."
>
> Especially disturbed was she at the full of the moon, and one could hear her wailing hymns at such times. The story is, too, that when Captain John Cook came home he pushed heavy furniture beside the door of his room because Mrs. Cook had the habit of honing the kitchen knives razor-sharp, as the knives of a whaling vessel are kept (Vorse, 22–23).

Mrs. Cook never fully recovered from the effects of the fateful winter in the Arctic and apparently suffered from severe depression. It has been reported that she became the subject of gossip among her neighbors in Provincetown. She died in 1922 at the age of 67 from heart failure. Shortly before her death, Captain Cook filed for divorce and married Ethel Sparks, the widow of his friend Captain Frederick Sparks. The incident became a town scandal and Captain Cook and his new wife moved to Florida, never returning to Provincetown.

Mary Heaton Vorse's prose version of the story, like O'Neill's theatrical one in *Ile*, suggested the creative emotions surging in Provincetown. Provincetown remained a creatively stimulating home for O'Neill for almost 10 years. During this time he completed 22 works, all of which were produced.

In the fall of 1917 O'Neill returned to New York. That season the Washington Square Players presented *In the Zone* and the Provincetown Players presented *The Long Voyage Home* and *Ile*. *The Long Voyage Home* also appeared in *The Smart Set* magazine. In the late fall, O'Neill met Agnes Boulton, a writer of magazine stories and novelettes. She was 24 at the time and had a daughter from a previous marriage, who lived with Agnes's mother in Connecticut. They met at the Hell Hole, a Greenwich Village bar that O'Neill had frequented for a few years. That winter Agnes accompanied O'Neill to Provincetown. O'Neill was earning some money at the time from a production of *In the Zone,* which was touring the vaudeville circuit.

In her memoir, *Part of A Long Story,* Agnes wrote that they traveled to Provincetown on the Fall River Line, which departed from the docks not far from Jimmy the Priest's. Ross Moffett, another member of the Provincetown artists' colony, recalled leaving New York on the Fall River Line at 5:00 P.M., "dined for all of eighty cents in the fancy varnished dining room, and awakened early the next morning with the steamer berthed in Fall River. At the dockside we took a train to the busy junction of Middleboro, where we finally caught the cars for Cape Cod" (Moffett, 29). Agnes referred to the last part of the trip as the "slow train that seemed to stop at every station on Cape Cod" (Boulton, 95).

In Provincetown, Eugene and Agnes were met by John Francis, O'Neill's landlord from the previous summer, who brought them to one of his flats. As Agnes recalled, after a few hours O'Neill exclaimed, "God! My God—how wonderful to be here!" She had never seen him so happy. They were married in Provincetown on 12 April.

Although he still drank heavily in New York, O'Neill abstained in dry Provincetown. Agnes wrote that O'Neill brought a pint of liquor with him from New York and was able to buy another pint in town. He used the two pints to help wean himself off alcohol and did not touch another drop for the next five months (Boulton, 99). That year he completed *Beyond the Horizon* and four one-act plays, including *The Rope* and *Where the Cross Is Made.*

Naval vessels at anchor in Provincetown harbor, ca. 1900 (Pilgrim Monument and Provincetown Museum)

Wartime Provincetown was busy with naval vessels and a lot of sailors in town. Shortly after the start of World War I Provincetown had become a naval station. And, indeed, the naval war was close in 1918. One day they heard the sound of gunfire, and the town was in a panic because a German U-boat had been seen near the harbor. Neither Agnes nor Eugene took the threat seriously (Boulton, 182). But it was not a false alarm. Mary Heaton Vorse wrote that on 21 July 1918 "there was a sound of gunfire and a siren sounded, which meant submarine attack" (Vorse, 132).

That day the German submarine, U-156, attacked the Lehigh Valley Railroad tug *Perth Amboy* and her string of four coal barges just off Orleans, about 15 miles south of Provincetown. All the barges were sunk and the tug was damaged, but the 31 people aboard the tug and barges escaped in their lifeboats, including tug captain Joe Tapley and his wife, two other women, and five children. Provincetown suffered other losses due to German U-boats. In August 1918 the *Annie C. Perry* of Provincetown, "once the queen of the fleet of fresh fishermen," was one of the fishing schooners destroyed by U-156 on the fishing grounds off Nova Scotia. Other former Provincetown boats sunk by U-boats included the local favorite *Rose Dorothea*, carrying salt from Portugal to Halifax (Vorse 136–37, Thomas, 113).

Agnes wrote many years later that the U-boat attacks along the coast did not have much impact on them. They certainly would have been aware, since their landlord and friend, John Francis, was instrumental in organizing aid for the survivors of the British steamship *Pennistone,* which was sunk by a U-boat off Provincetown. O'Neill's play *In the Zone* deals with the threat of the war and U-boats, but it was written the year before, illustrating the broad psychological threat presented by U-boats from the outset of the war.

As he had since his recovery from tuberculosis, O'Neill liked to take long swims and lie in the hot sand when he took a break from his writing. He and Agnes began to discuss spending future summers somewhere other than in Francis's flat because it was "too near civilization to really suit him" (Boulton, 171). On one occasion they went out to the old Life-Saving Service station at Peaked Hill Bars, several miles from Provincetown, which had been turned into a summer home. Sand had drifted against the house up to the roof, and they were able to climb up and sit in the lookout. As they looked out over the ocean, O'Neill said to her: "This is the house you and I should have! We would live here like sea gulls, two sea gulls coming home at night to our home" (Boulton, 181–82).

The Peaked Hill Bars station and the neighboring Race Point station —both built in 1872—were the first two stations established near Provincetown. But once the sea eroded the shore nearby, the Peaked Hill Bars station had been replaced by a new station of the same name, about a half mile away, in 1914. Meanwhile, the dunes naturally rebuilt themselves and the former station survived. Sam Lewisohn, a New York financier, bought the station from the government and converted it into a home.

In the fall of 1918, John Francis—acting as agent for Lewisohn—let O'Neill know that the house was for sale. Mabel Dodge, a member of the

Greenwich Village crowd, had furnished the house for Lewisohn. Dodge and Lewisohn alternated their use of the house in the summer (Sheaffer, SP, 435). O'Neill offered to make a partial payment on the property and pay the rest over time, but Lewisohn wanted the full price of the house up front. O'Neill could not afford it and decided that they would settle on renting something smaller the following summer season.

In November, O'Neill and Agnes prepared to return to New York. They had stayed in Provincetown longer than most of the other seasonal residents. According to Agnes, O'Neill did not want to leave, and he turned sullen (Boulton, 219). However, *Where the Cross Is Made* was going into rehearsal for the Provincetown Players production in the city. That winter they lived in a house that Agnes owned in West Point Pleasant, New Jersey, not far from the ocean and with train service to New York City.

**The Peaked Hill Bars Life-Saving Station converted into a home
(Sheaffer–O'Neill Collection, Connecticut College)**

Peaked Hill Bars,
Bermuda, and Beyond

"The Atlantic for a front lawn, miles of sand dunes for a back yard. . . . "

—Eugene O'Neill to George C. Tyler, 8 June 1919 (Bogard, 90)

Late in the fall of 1918, O'Neill spoke to his father about the Peaked Hill Bars property. James decided to buy the former Coast Guard station for his son and his new wife as a wedding present. The relationship between O'Neill and his father had greatly improved since the younger O'Neill had finally settled into a line of work and was displaying promise. With new respect for his son, and approving of his marriage, James began negotiations in secret. John Francis's correspondence with Eugene O'Neill and the owner of the property indicates that negotiations continued from December 1918 through the following March, when the sale was completed. The cost of the house, with its contents and outbuildings, was $1,000.

James O'Neill sold some of his property in New London to obtain the cash for the Peaked Hill purchase. The New London transactions were delayed due to James's health, which in turn delayed the Peaked Hill purchase. In a letter to Francis, O'Neill described his father's situation: "An automobile nudged him in the rear as he was crossing Fifth Avenue and gave him a bad knock to the pavement. It is only the mercy of God that he was not killed. As it was he suffered severely from shock and one of his legs is still in such bad shape that up to date he hasn't been able to leave the apartment; so of course he hasn't been able to take the journey to New London to wind up the real estate deal I wrote to you about in my last letter."[39] James recovered from the accident, but he realized that in general his health was declining. Later that year, James also sold the Monte Cristo Cottage and the adjacent New London property and had his other properties transferred to Ella's name.

According to Agnes, she and O'Neill traveled to Provincetown in March 1919 with the expectation of spending the summer in a rental.

John Francis met them at the train station and, to their surprise, informed them that James O'Neill had bought the Peaked Hill house for them. In a letter to Francis regarding the property, dated 8 March 1919, O'Neill revealed the strength of his bond to Provincetown: "I filled in Province-town as my residence. As I was married there under that understanding, and as I have lived there the greater part of the last three years, I think I may justly regard it as my home town—(if I ever had any!)."[40]

The Eugene O'Neills looked forward to their first summer at Peaked Hill Bars. Agnes wrote about their anticipation of "lying in the sun, swimming, watching the sea and the ships that went along the hori-zon" (Boulton, 311). They were staying in town while the sand was cleared from around the house and other preparations were made. In May of 1919 O'Neill and Agnes moved to their new home. The house was about two and a half miles from the village of Provincetown. The only access was across the sand dunes, which have been described as "the great sand deserts" (Dalton, 74). The house was as "solitary as a ship, overlooking the sea" (Sheaffer, SP, 455).

The O'Neills' only neighbors were the Coast Guard crew at the sta-tion half a mile away. The station was staffed by the keeper or captain year round, joined by his crew of seven from September through June. The Coast Guard crew delivered the occasional phone message and mail and saw the O'Neills while they were on their patrols. They were the type of men O'Neill would have enjoyed, probably not unlike the crew of the *Charles Racine*. Many had been to sea before joining the Life-Saving Service or Coast Guard. They had experience as whalemen or fishermen under sail, and were expert boat-handlers as well. O'Neill's association with the crew more than likely fed and reinforced his fascination and romantic view of the age of sail, and it is evident that the crew enjoyed O'Neill as well. He was known to them before he moved to Peaked Hill Bars, probably due to his long walks on the outer shore over the previous couple of years. They presented O'Neill with a desk that they had made from ships' timbers they salvaged from wrecks along the shore.

Agnes had not seen the interior of the house until the day they moved in, and she found it still strongly redolent of lifesaving. For more than 40 years it had been a base of operation for lifesavers, a place of refuge for shipwrecked sailors in a storm, and a temporary resting place

Surfboat and men of the Coast Guard's Peaked Hill Bars Station, ca. 1920 (Pilgrim Monument and Provincetown Museum)

for bodies pulled from the sea. The boat room was now the living room, the galley used by the station crew was the dining room, and the bunk room upstairs continued to be bedrooms (Breese, 72). In an interview for *Bookman* in 1921 O'Neill said: "The stairs are like companionways of a ship. There are lockers everywhere. . . . The big boat room, now our living room, still has steel fixtures in the ceiling from which one of the boats was slung. . . . The look-out station on the roof is the same as when the Coast Guards spent their external two-hour vigils there" (Sheaffer, SP, 457). The lookout position on the top of the house provided views of the open sea, the long stretch of the sandy coastline, and the rolling dunes. O'Neill boasted that he had the Atlantic Ocean for a front yard and miles of sand dunes for his back yard (Bowen, 111). O'Neill's study was on the second floor, facing the sea. He did most of his writing on an oversized bunk, but he also had the large desk presented to him by the Coast Guardsmen. Harry Kemp, who spent many summers in a shack among the dunes in Provincetown, described the view:

> The sunrises are enormous, spraying the east with unimagined colors. . . . when there are clouds, they march like cities moving, in whatever direction the wind blows. Out in the ocean a strange life goes on. Porpoises roll and sport. Herds

of fish drive this way and that. . . . Whales are often seen. . . .
In the back, in the heart of the dune-country, there is a petri-
fied forest buried. Bone-white sand-carved bits of wood and
what were once greening branches work up through the
sand (Sheaffer, SP, 456).

Their remote location on the edge of the sea and their role in life-and-
death struggles imbued these stations with almost supernatural aura for
O'Neill's Provincetown writer acquaintances. Mary Heaton Vorse recalled a story told to her by William Cook (no relation to Captain John
Cook, the inspiration for *Ile*) who had been keeper of the Peaked Hill Bars
Station from 1897 until his retirement in 1915 at age 64. While making his
rounds one night, one of the surfmen was surprised to meet a girl in the
fog. The next night he saw her again. Stirred by her beauty he begged to
meet her again. She said that they would meet again soon. A few nights
later a Portuguese ship stranded on Peaked Hill Bars. As the surfboat
approached, the surfman saw the girl on deck with a baby in her arms.
She waved to him, and as the boat pulled alongside she threw the baby to
him. She then jumped, but missed the boat and fell into the sea and was
lost. The man realized that it had been her spirit he had met on previous
nights, and that she was giving him her daughter. The surfman later
adopted the orphan girl (Vorse, 57).

In another Peaked Hill Bars legend, a white stallion swam ashore
from a wrecked ship, the only survivor. Men on shore tried to catch the
stallion, without any luck, until they put a mare in an enclosure and
trapped him. The stallion leaped the fence and the men cornered the
horse on the beach. As they approached, the horse "plunged furiously
into the sea . . . defying them to capture him and preferring death to captivity." Vorse explained: "When I first came here the old coast guard still
spoke of the waves as white horses" (Vorse, 194).

Stories such as these may seem far-fetched, but they had some resonance for O'Neill. He often said that the ideal way to die would be to
swim out to sea until he could not swim any further, and be swallowed by
the sea. As maudlin as this may sound, O'Neill's passion for the sea and
swimming in it could be interpreted as a natural choice, an escape from
captivity and a finding of freedom in death, the choice of the stallion. In
1921 O'Neill said:

I feel a true kinship and harmony with life out there. Sand and sun and sea and wind—you merge into them, and become as meaningless and as full of meaning as they are. There is always the monotone of surf on the bar—a background for silence—and you *know* that you are alone. . . . You can walk or swim along the beach for miles, and meet only the dunes—Sphinxes muffled in their yellow robes with paws deep in the sea (Sheaffer, SP, 456).

Some of the men from the Peaked Hill Bars Station had become local legends as well. Captain David H. Atkins, Frank A. Mayo, and Elisha Taylor were lost during the rescue of the crew of the *C. E. Trumbull* in 1880, described earlier. O'Neill used the names Atkins and Mayo for the family names in *Beyond the Horizon,* which he wrote in 1918 while living in Provincetown.

O'Neill continued his accustomed work pattern at Peaked Hill Bars, writing in the morning, taking a long swim in the afternoon, and

O'Neill seated at the desk made for him by the neighboring Coast Guard crew (Sheaffer-O'Neill Collection, Connecticut College)

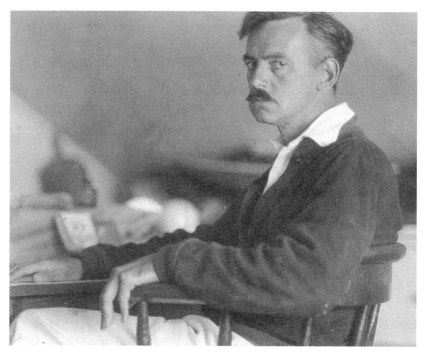

then writing again. Many of O'Neill's contemporaries commented on his long swims. Agnes wrote about watching her husband swimming and noticing a second head swimming alongside him. When O'Neill returned from the water he told her that a seal had swum with him. The seal remained in the area for several days and continued to swim with O'Neill (Boulton, 319–20). Jerry Farnsworth, an artist, remembered that after a nor'easter there was terrific surf and no one would go near the water. But O'Neill was "like a creature of the sea" doing the back-stroke (Sheaffer, SP, 458). Hazel Hawthorne recalled walking along the beach while O'Neill "would be idling by in the sea when I passed on shore, and would raise an arm in greeting with a flash of a smile that I never saw when he was ashore" (Sheaffer, SA, 25). Mary Heaton Vorse wrote: "You knew more about him when you saw him swim. He swam like a South Sea Islander" (Vorse, 122).

O'Neill also began to kayak while at Peaked Hill Bars, and loved it almost as much as swimming. According to Harry Kemp, on one of O'Neill's forays in his kayak he was about five miles out and came along-side a fishing schooner. The captain yelled at him, "You git back to shore as quick as you can, you crazy loon!" (Sheaffer, SP, 458). At times he would go around the tip of Cape Cod and paddle into Provincetown harbor, a trip that is more than 10 miles by sea in one direction.

On occasion things washed up on the O'Neills' beach. One night during a storm a cat was howling outside their door. They saw that a barge had washed up on the beach, apparently having broken loose from its tow. The cat was the only survivor, which the O'Neills adopted and named Anna Christie (Boulton, 207).

On another occasion O'Neill saw a five-gallon kerosene tin wash-ing ashore. It contained pure alcohol. Apparently it had been dumped by a rumrunner that was pursued by the Coast Guard the night before. The O'Neills salvaged about a dozen tins altogether (Boulton, 307).

It is clear that during his years at Peaked Hill Bars O'Neill went from being a beginning playwright to a seasoned professional. It was one of the most productive periods in his life. The first year they owned the house at Peaked Hill Bars O'Neill completed *The Straw*, inspired by his time at Gaylord Farm Sanatorium, *Chris Christophersen*, and three one-act plays that he later destroyed. O'Neill found the isolation of the outer

**O'Neill, Shane, and Agnes on the dunes at Peaked Hill Bars, ca. 1922
(Sheaffer–O'Neill Collection, Connecticut College)**

Cape an ideal place to write, completing approximately 24 plays that would go on to be produced. Broadway producer George C. Tyler optioned *Chris Christophersen* with the idea of bringing it to New York. Tyler had been James O'Neill's producer and the man through whom O'Neill received his allowance while he lived at Jimmy the Priest's.

The year was eventful in other ways. Agnes was expecting their first child. By the end of the summer they moved into a cottage in town, owned by John Francis, to make things easier and more comfortable for Agnes. Shane, O'Neill's second son and first child of this marriage, was born on 30 October 1919.

In February 1920, *Beyond the Horizon* opened in New York to great critical praise. During the winter, *Chris Christophersen* tried out in Philadelphia and Atlantic City, but Tyler decided not to bring it to New York and the production closed out of town. O'Neill had been in New York while the plays were in rehearsal, and in late winter he returned to Provincetown, where he completed *Gold,* a reworking and lengthening of *Where the Cross Is Made.*

Around the same time James O'Neill had a stroke. When the doctors discovered that he had intestinal cancer, he requested to be transferred to the Lawrence and Memorial Associated Hospitals in New London in June. He wanted to return to the community where he had spent most of his summers for 35 years (Black, 259). Eugene went to New London to be with his parents and brother Jamie, and was there in August when James died and was buried at St. Mary's Cemetery in New London. James had lived long enough to see his son win his first Pulitzer Prize, for *Beyond the Horizon.*

After his father's death, O'Neill wrote six plays in 18 months. Stephen Black attributes this amazing productivity to a "creative upwelling" in reaction to his father's death. The inspiring and isolated environment of Provincetown continued to be a nurturing atmosphere for his creative expression. He revised *Chris Christophersen,* which became *"Anna Christie"* and went on to write *The Emperor Jones* and *Diff'rent.* The following year (1921) he completed drafts of *The First Man* and *The Fountain,* and by the end of the year he finished *The Hairy Ape.* That year O'Neill saw an unsuccessful run of *Gold* and a successful run of *"Anna Christie"* on Broadway. When he was in New York in the fall for rehearsals of *"Anna Christie"* he met his son Eugene Jr. for the first time.

The year of 1922 brought more success and tragedy. Since the death of her husband, Ella O'Neill had been living in San Francisco, assisted by Jamie, who had gotten his alcoholism under control since his father's death. But Ella suffered a series of strokes and died. Jamie brought the body east to lie beside James in St. Mary's Cemetery in New London. In a nice piece of irony, they arrived in New York on 9 March, the night the Provincetown Players opened their production of *The Hairy Ape*.

That spring the production of *The Hairy Ape* moved to Broadway for a successful run, and O'Neill received his second Pulitzer Prize, for *"Anna Christie."* During the summer Eugene Jr. visited his father for the first time at Peaked Hill Bars.

In a few short years O'Neill's family had begun to grow, with the birth of Shane and the entry into his life of Eugene Jr., and also experienced loss, with the death of O'Neill's parents and the decline of his brother Jamie. After their mother's death, Jamie again turned to alcohol and would die in a sanatorium in New Jersey in November 1923. The playwright was also experiencing great professional success and was finally able to support himself and his family. In the fall of 1922, O'Neill and Agnes purchased Brook Farm, a 32-acre property in Ridgefield, Connecticut. Agnes managed the fields and orchards at Brook Farm "compe-

Eugene Jr., Agnes, and O'Neill on the beach at Peaked Hill Bars (Sheaffer-O'Neill Collection, Connecticut College)

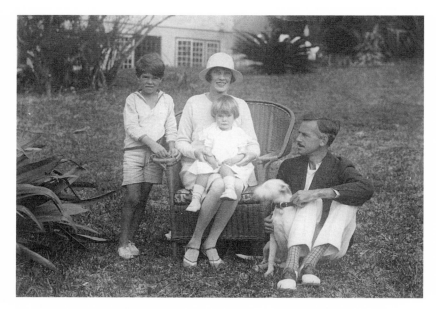

Shane, Agnes, Oona, and O'Neill in Bermuda, ca. 1927 (Sheaffer–O'Neill Collection, Connecticut College)

O'Neill kayaking in Bermuda, ca. 1927 (Sheaffer–O'Neill Collection, Connecticut College)

tently and energetically" (Black, 296). They lived at Brook Farm in winter and continued to summer at Peaked Hill Bars.

By this time O'Neill was recognizing that he did his most productive writing in the warm months. He was generally in a better state of mind when he had the sun, the beach, and the opportunity to swim (Sheaffer, SA, 154). His winters at Brook Farm had not been productive. So, in November 1924 O'Neill and his family sailed to Bermuda for the winter. They rented two cottages in a thickly wooded area that led down to cliffs overlooking the sea and a long stretch of beach. One of the cottages was reserved for O'Neill to write. From Bermuda, O'Neill wrote to his old landlord and friend, John Francis, in Provincetown: "Swimming every day in the ocean! Never again any cold for me! I love Provincetown in the spring, summer & fall—but that's all!"[41] In Bermuda, O'Neill had the sun, sand, and sea close at hand, just as at Peaked Hill Bars. In May 1925 his daughter Oona was born.

That summer the magic of Peaked Hill Bars began to dissipate. Provincetown was becoming a more populated summer community. According to Mary Heaton Vorse, "The old life whose pace was slow and easy, like the tide coming in, lasted until 1920. Now it was gone. . . . The summer crowd had come to stay" (Vorse, 183). As O'Neill's celebrity grew, hopeful writers, students, and simply curious tourists hiked across the dunes to Peaked Hill Bars "to pay their respect as if they were pilgrims," Mary Heaton Vorse recalled. "Gene didn't like it. Eventually, this sort of thing caused him to leave Provincetown" (Bowen, 128).

O'Neill no longer had the solitude he once had, and the temptation to drink had increased. His writing suffered, as it always did when he was drinking. Seeking a change, the O'Neills went to Nantucket that summer, and the following summer to Belgrade Lakes in Maine instead of Peaked Hill Bars.

They purchased a piece of property called Spithead in Bermuda in 1926. Located on a private harbor once the base for privateers who preyed on French and Spanish merchant ships, the property included the shell of an eighteenth-century house and another house that needed repair but was more immediately habitable.

O'Neill was becoming restless in his relationship as well. In 1927 he began traveling back and forth to New York while Agnes and the children

O'Neill and Carlotta on Long Island, 1931 (Sheaffer-O'Neill Collection, Connecticut College)

remained in Bermuda. He became reacquainted with Carlotta Monterey, who had played Mildred in *The Hairy Ape* on Broadway, and they began an affair. Carlotta was the same age as O'Neill, and she had a child from one of her previous marriages, who lived on the West Coast with Carlotta's mother. In February of 1928, without informing Agnes who was still in Bermuda, O'Neill and Carlotta left for Europe. In October, O'Neill and Carlotta embarked on a trip to China, returning to France in January 1929. They rented a villa on the Riviera and then in June moved to a chateau near Tours.

O'Neill had been in contact with Agnes to discuss the possibility of a divorce. She agreed and obtained one in early July of 1929 in Reno, Nevada, where the laws made divorce easier to obtain than in other parts of the country. In the settlement, Agnes received Spithead and alimony. Carlotta became O'Neill's third wife later that month. O'Neill maintained ownership of the Peaked Hill Bars house until he gave it to Eugene Jr. in 1930. At the time he wrote to his son, "That place meant a lot to me . . . as a solitude where I lived with myself it had infinite meaning" (Egan, x). But the dunes finally eroded away and the house fell into the sea in January 1931.

With his departure from Peaked Hill Bars, the themes of O'Neill's plays moved away from maritime inspirations, with the exception of

Mourning Becomes Electra and "The Calms of Capricorn." He began *Mourning Becomes Electra* in 1929 and finished it the following year. "The Calms of Capricorn" was the fifth play in a nine-play cycle about a New England family, which he started working on in 1934. The only element of "The Calms of Capricorn" that survives is a scenario along with some of O'Neill's drawings of the set. The play was to take place in 1857, on a clipper ship in Boston Harbor and at sea, bound for San Francisco. Of the other plays in the cycle, he completed *A Touch of the Poet* and a draft of *More Stately Mansions*.

Even though O'Neill had stopped writing about the sea and the people tied to that world, he still found the need to live near water. In 1932 he and Carlotta had a house built at Sea Island, Georgia. They named it Casa Genotta, combining their names, Gene and Carlotta. The house was modeled after old Spanish farmhouses, although O'Neill's study recalled a captain's cabin on a sailing ship, with oak ribs and a beamed ceiling. In the center was the representation of a mast encircled with belaying pins, and the bay of windows suggested the stern of a galleon. A circular iron stairway, as in a lighthouse led to a rooftop lookout, like that of a life-saving station, overlooking a wide sweep of beach. According to Carlotta, eventually O'Neill grew tired of his study, thinking it felt too much like a stage set (Sheaffer, SA, 397). They sold the house in 1937.

O'Neill and Carlotta moved to the West Coast in the fall of 1936 and, for three months, rented a house in Seattle on a bluff overlooking Puget Sound. There, O'Neill learned that he had won the Noble Prize for Literature. From Seattle they moved to Carlotta's hometown of San Francisco, and before long bought property in Danville, California, where they built Tao House in 1937. It was one of the few homes for O'Neill that was not near the sea, but it is where he wrote *Long Day's Journey into Night* and *The Iceman Cometh*. They stayed there until 1944, when they moved to San Francisco and then in 1945 moved back to an apartment in New York City.

Eugene and Carlotta began looking for a new home in the vicinity of Boston in 1948. They had already looked in Provincetown, but they did not like the atmosphere of a tourist town (Bowen, 342). They found a small cottage in Marblehead, on the North Shore of Massachusetts. It faced the sea, but to Carlotta their new home, compared to Casa Genotta

O'Neill at his home in Marblehead (Sheaffer–O'Neill Collection, Connecticut College)

and Tao House, was like "a birdcage," while O'Neill was reminded of his family's first home, the Monte Cristo Cottage. Being so close to the sea, O'Neill felt that he would be able to write again (Sheaffer, SA, 613). As early as the mid-1930s O'Neill had developed a tremor in his hand that made it difficult to write. As the years progressed the tremor intensified to a point that he was unable to write. He tried dictation and other techniques to get his thoughts down on paper, but he was most successful at creating plays by physically putting a pencil to paper. By 1951 his health declined further. They sold the Marblehead house and moved to a residential hotel in Boston, overlooking the Charles River. O'Neill was frustrated by the fact that his mind remained active but he could not control his body. The river provided him with a connection to the sea, and he sat and watched the sailboats and sculls on the river. He died in the hotel from pneumonia on 27 November 1953 at the age of 65.

In 1927 Susan Glaspell wrote about the opening night of *Bound East for Cardiff* back in 1916: "The sea has been good to Eugene O'Neill. It was there for his opening. There was a fog, just as the script demanded, fog bell in the harbor. The tide was in, and it washed under us and around, spraying through the holes in the floor, giving us the rhythm and flavor of the sea while the big dying sailor talked to his friend Drisc of the life he had always wanted deep in land, where you'd never see a ship or smell the sea" (Deutsch, 12).

The sea indeed had been good to O'Neill and throughout his life he kept returning to it. It provided him more than just material for his plays. The sea provided solace, inspiration, and a home.

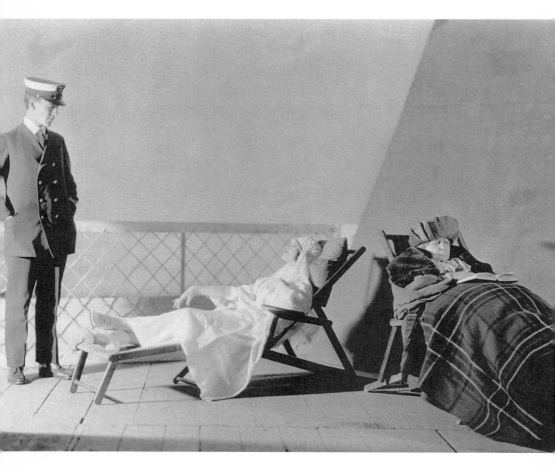

1922 production of *The Hairy Ape* **with Carlotta Monterey (center)
(Sheaffer–O'Neill Collection, Connecticut College)**

The Plays

O'Neill's youth in New London and the two years he was immersed in the world of maritime laborers profoundly affected his life and work. Given his powers of observation, it is not surprising that he held on to details, but it was necessary for him to have time for reflection before he could gain perspective and arrive at some clarity of purpose.

That time came without warning, when in December of 1912, at the age of 24, he was diagnosed with tuberculosis and entered Gaylord Farm Sanatorium for treatment. "At Gaylord I really *thought about* my life for the first time, about past and future," he would reflect later. "Undoubtedly the inactivity forced upon me by life at a san[atorium] forced me to mental activity especially as I had always been high-strung and nervous temperamentally" (Sheaffer, SP, 252).

O'Neill's time at Gaylord came shortly after his sojourn in the sailor's world. Its marked effect materialized in his early writing, particularly the maritime related work: *Fog, Thirst, Warnings*, the Glencairn plays (*Bound East for Cardiff, The Long Voyage Home, The Moon of the Caribbees,* and *In The Zone*), *The Personal Equation, Ile, Where the Cross Is Made, Gold, The Rope*, the short story "Tomorrow," *Chris Christophersen, Beyond the Horizon, "Anna Christie,"* and *The Hairy Ape*. All of these plays were written between 1913 and 1921. O'Neill's maritime influences continued to play themselves out in some of his later work as well, including *Mourning Becomes Electra* and his ideas for "The Calms of Capricorn." New London and Provincetown, with their reliance on and proximity to the sea, were a steady backdrop and significant inspiration for his creative endeavors. And the realism that he drew out of his maritime experiences and settings put him in the forefront of the development of a unique style of American theater.

THIRST, WARNINGS, AND FOG

Even as he committed himself to becoming a playwright, Eugene O'Neill had much to learn. Nevertheless, his years of being on the road with his father, watching innumerable productions from backstage and from the front of the house, seeing rehearsals, and socializing with actors and actresses had taught him much about the art of the theater. In addition, his own incisive observations of his life experiences gave him strong settings—especially in the maritime world—for his plays. These aspects of his developing craft are seen in *Thirst* and *Warnings*, written in 1913, and *Fog*, written in 1914. These three works were included in *Thirst and Other One Act Plays*, published in 1914, when O'Neill was 24, in a volume financed by his father.

The three plays all deal with shipwrecks. *Thirst* and *Fog* are about people adrift in lifeboats after their liner has sunk, while *Warnings* ends with the sinking of the ship. O'Neill exploits the drama inherent in a shipwreck, but Sheaffer points out that the theme can be viewed psychologically as well, with the ship representing a mother figure and the individuals adrift on the open sea the children who are cut off from their mother (Sheaffer, SP, 271). O'Neill certainly had the basis for both conscious and subconscious thoughts of separation from his mother because of her morphine addiction and the years he spent in boarding school.

The idea of the ship as a mother and her boats as children would not have been unfamiliar to him, given his youth in New London and his time at sea. But the fear of being on a sinking ship or being set adrift was something O'Neill must have felt during his time on the *Charles Racine* in a hurricane. The realization of the risk was made clear to O'Neill and the public at large when the 1,000-foot transatlantic liner *Titanic* sank in April 1912 with the loss of 1,503. On its maiden voyage from Southampton, England, to New York City, the "unsinkable" *Titanic* struck an iceberg south of the Grand Banks. Without enough lifeboats for all on board, and in the chaos of the ship's settling in the frigid waters, relatively few boats got away in good order, while passengers stampeded about the decks and some seemed to deny their doom by fixating on unimportant details. Less than a year earlier, O'Neill had traveled the same route aboard the *Philadelphia* and had spent time on watch in the crow's nest looking out for hazards. Even though the setting of the plays went a step beyond his own experience, they were grounded in his observations, not solely on his imagination.

Thirst is set on a steamer's life raft adrift on a tropical sea, being circled by sharks. O'Neill lists the characters in the raft as Gentleman, Dancer, and West Indian Mulatto Sailor. All three are dying of thirst, but the Gentleman and Dancer think that the Sailor has some drinking water hidden. The Dancer offers the Sailor her diamond necklace and then her body in exchange for some water. The Sailor has no water to give. When the Dancer dies from thirst, the Sailor takes out his knife, indicating he is going to eat her to satisfy his hunger and thirst. The Gentleman is horrified and pushes her body into the sea. The Sailor stabs the Gentleman, who falls back into the sea, pulling the Sailor in with him, and they are taken by the sharks. The play closes with the diamond necklace glittering in the sunshine.

O'Neill draws on his experiences aboard the *Charles Racine* in a number of instances. The opening stage direction reflects the isolation when the *Racine* was becalmed:

> A steamer's life raft rising and falling slowly on the long ground-swell of a glassy tropic sea. The sky above is pitilessly clear, of a steel blue color merging into black shadow on the horizon's rim. The sun glares down from straight overhead like a great angry eye of God. The heat is terrific. Writhing, fantastic heatwaves rise from the white deck of the raft. Here and there on the still surface of the sea the fins of sharks may be seen slowly cutting the surface of the water in lazy circles (O'Neill, CP1, 31).

Through the Sailor, O'Neill reveals what he learned from the crew of the *Racine* about their superstitions and their fear and loathing of sharks. At the opening of the play, the Sailor sings a monotonous song as he watches the sharks circle. When he is asked what the song means the sailor says, while pointing at the sharks: "I am singing to them. It is a charm. I have been told it is very strong. If I sing long enough they will not eat us" (O'Neill, CP1, 34). In a moment of irony the Gentleman pulls a folded card from his pocket, looks at it, and laughs. The Dancer asks him why he's laughing. He explains that it is a souvenir program menu from a banquet held in his honor at the United States Club in Buenos Aires—a side of the port that O'Neill had not experienced. He reads the menu to her: "Martini cocktails, soup, sherry, fish, Burgundy, chicken, champagne." He continues laughing madly and says: "here we are dying for a crust of bread, for a drink of water!" (O'Neill, CP1, 37–38).

O'Neill likely used the reports and survivor accounts from the *Titanic* for the Dancer's and Gentleman's descriptions of what happened as their ship sank. The Dancer recalls being on deck:

> Everywhere they were fighting to get into the boats. This poor little man stood by himself. His moon face was convulsed with rage. He kept repeating in loud angry tones: "I shall be late. I must cable! I can never make it!" He was still bewailing his broken appointment when a rush of the crowd swept him off his feet and into the sea. I can see him now. He is the only person besides the Captain I remember clearly (O'Neill, CP1, 38).

The Gentleman tells her his recollection:

> Then the crash came—that horrible dull crash. We were all thrown forward on the floor of the salon; then screams, oaths, fainting women, the hollow boom of a bulkhead giving way. I vaguely remember rushing to my stateroom and picking up my wallet. It must have been that menu I took instead. Then I was on deck fighting in the midst of the crowd. Somehow I got into a boat—but it was overloaded and was swamped immediately. I swam to another boat. They beat me off with oars. That boat too was swamped a moment later. And then the gurgling, choking cries of the drowning! Something huge rushed by me in the water leaving a gleaming trail of phosphorescence. A woman near me with a life belt around her gave a cry of agony and disappeared—then I realized—sharks! I became frenzied with terror. I swam. I beat the water with my hands. The ship had gone down. I swam and swam with but one idea—to put all that horror behind me. I saw something white on the water before me. I clutched it—climbed on it. It was this raft. You and he were on it. I fainted (O'Neill, CP1, 39).

The Gentleman questions the Dancer on how she came to be on the raft with the Sailor and no one else. She cannot recall how it happened. One of the last things she remembers is being given a kiss on deck before she fainted. She says:

> You remember the Second Officer—the young Englishman with the great dark eyes who was so tall and handsome? All the women loved him. I, too, I loved him—a little bit. He loved me—very much—so he said. Yes, I know he loved me very much. I think it was he who kissed me. I am almost sure it was he (O'Neill, CP1, 41).

They continue to discuss the fact that it must have been the Second Officer who got her into the raft after she had fainted. In a combination of wish and reality, O'Neill modeled the character of the Second Officer after himself. He was tall, handsome, with dark eyes, and he was loved by many women. He had had many liaisons with dancers and actresses during his days in New York City, particularly the year he attended Princeton. The women of those years were likely the inspiration for the Dancer.

O'Neill went on to use a character of Second Officer, Second Engineer, or Second Mate in a number of plays, including *The Personal Equation* (which was originally titled "The Second Engineer"), *Ile*, *Chris Christophersen*, *The Hairy Ape*, and *Bound East for Cardiff*. In several instances O'Neill's description of the characters of Second Officer or Engineer reflect himself. On stage, O'Neill appeared in the original productions of two of his plays: as the Second Mate in *Bound East for Cardiff*, and as the Sailor in *Thirst*. Both productions were during O'Neill's first season with The Provincetown Players.

The one-act play *Warnings* is about a steamship wireless operator named James Knapp, who learns that he is losing his hearing and could become completely deaf at any time. He knows that he should give up his job. But, driven by the need to earn money for his family, he decides that he will go to sea one more time. His ship runs into a derelict vessel and begins to sink. Knapp sends messages asking for help, but he gets no response. Later it is revealed that because of his hearing loss he had not heard earlier wireless warnings from other ships about the derelict vessel. The tragic mishap could have been avoided if he had heard the warnings. The play concludes with Knapp's suicide.

The play has two scenes. The first takes place in James Knapp's dining room in the Bronx, and the second aboard Knapp's ship, the

"SS *Empress*." The characters in Scene One include Mrs. Knapp and their five children, who range in age from one to fifteen. The scene opens with a frenzy of familial activity presided over by the mother: the middle children bickering, concerns about waking the baby, and the two oldest children arriving home full of energy and excitement. The household has all the chaotic normalcy of an average family. This was not the home life that O'Neill had experienced in his youth, but it was similar to Mrs. Rippin's handling of her family. O'Neill wrote the play in 1913, and in the fall of that year he started to board with the Rippins. It is likely that he wrote the play while living there. In any event, he knew the family and their household well enough since the O'Neills had taken many of their meals at the Rippins'. Stephen Black suggests that O'Neill modeled the character of Knapp after his own father, a man who is haunted by poverty and unable to stop working (Black, 149). The Gelbs mention another possible source for Knapp, a fellow roomer at Jimmy the Priest's, nicknamed "the Lunger." They refer to him as "a broken-down telegrapher" and report that he tried to teach O'Neill the International Code (Gelb, LWMC, 295).

Stories related to the loss of the *Titanic* and the ensuing inquiries may well have been the source of O'Neill's inspiration for *Warnings*. It was discovered, after the fact, that the steamer *Californian* was less than 20 miles from the *Titanic* when she began to sink. The *Californian* was unaware of the vessel in distress as no radio operator was on duty that night. In the aftermath of the *Titanic* disaster, legislation required that vessels have a radio operator on duty around the clock.

As with most of O'Neill's plays, his stage directions for *Warnings* are very precise and descriptive. He provides minute detail as if he were describing actual places. His shipboard or sailor influences are evident in the opening description of Scene Two:

> A section of the boat deck of the SS *Empress* just abaft of the bridge. The deck slants sharply downward in the direction of the bow. To the left the officers' cabins with several lighted port holes. Just in back of them and in the middle of the deck is the wireless room with its door wide open revealing James Knapp bent over his instrument on the forward side of the compartment (O'Neill, CP1, 88).

In addition to the details of the ship, evident here is O'Neill's familiarity with a sailor's vocabulary. He uses the word "abaft," meaning behind, and "forward," towards the bow or front end of the ship. At the close of the play, when they are abandoning ship, Knapp realizes he is responsible for what has happened, and he shoots himself. A shipmate rushes in to see what is keeping Knapp and discovers Knapp's suicide. In the stage directions O'Neill says: "He gives one horrified glance at the body in the room; says 'Good God!' in a stupefied tone, and then, seized with sudden terror, rushes astern again" (O'Neill, CP1, 94)—"astern" meaning to the stern or back end of the ship to a sailor. Throughout his sea-related plays, O'Neill's descriptions of the sailor's environment and its vocabulary provide authenticity and show clearly how much O'Neill understood of that world.

Like *Thirst,* the third play, *Fog,* takes place on a life raft adrift at sea. The latter play is set in the North Atlantic near the Grand Banks. The play bears a similarity to *Warnings* in that the characters are adrift because their ship sank after colliding with a derelict vessel. The opening dialogue is about the fact that help must be on the way because the wireless operator must have sent numerous distress messages. *Fog* is not as naturalistic as *Thirst* and *Warnings.* In the play, O'Neill experiments with expressionism. The principal characters are a Poet, Man of Business, Polish Peasant Woman, and her Dead Child. The Peasant Woman never speaks—she is asleep in the raft throughout the play. O'Neill lists the Dead Child as a character, but the child has died before the play begins.

The life raft is adrift in a thick fog and comes close to an iceberg. There is the sound of a steamer in the distance. The Man of Business wants to call out for help, but the Poet will not let him, afraid that the steamer might strike the iceberg and sink. As the fog lifts they see the steamer, and one of its boats comes alongside the raft. The officer in command of the boat explains that the sound of a crying child guided them to the life raft. The Poet says the child has been dead for 24 hours. They then discover that the woman has died in her sleep.

The major theme of the play is selfishness and greed versus idealism, ultimately represented all too broadly in the names of the vocal characters. The Business Man wants to call out to the ship, hoping for rescue, but gives no thought to the peril into which that might place the steamer.

The Poet also wants to be rescued, but he is willing to take the chance of forfeiting his life rather than put the steamer in danger.

Impressionistically, O'Neill's script identifications for the characters change as the play progresses. At the opening of the play the script identifies the male characters as simply "First Voice" and "Second Voice." But as the fog begins to lift the characters become revealed more fully, both in the manner in which they are identified in the text and in the way O'Neill describes them in the stage directions. The "Second Voice" becomes the "Dark Man" and then "The Poet." The "First Voice" becomes the "Other Man" and is finally revealed as "The Business Man." The stage directions say:

> The faces of the two men in the boat can be dimly distinguished—one round, jowly, and clean shaven; the other oval with big dark eyes and a black moustache and black hair pushed back from his high forehead (O'Neill, CP1, 101).

Again, O'Neill is using himself for one of the characters, the Dark Man, later revealed as the Poet. For the Businessman, O'Neill quite likely used as his model one of New London's well-to-do business figures, or Casino members, with whom he had conflicts.

O'Neill makes reference to New London and his familiarity with its shore, and at the same time summons up a reminder of the *Titanic:*

> FIRST VOICE: Oh, this'll all go away as soon as the sun goes up. I've seen plenty like it at my country place on the Connecticut shore, maybe not as thick as this one but nearly as bad and when the sun came up they always disappeared before morning was over.
>
> SECOND VOICE: You forget we are now near the Grand Banks, the home of fog (O'Neill, CP1, 98).

O'Neill certainly understood the nature of fog from his youth in New London. His reference to the Grand Banks being "the home of fog" comes from a variety of sources: Kipling's *Captains Courageous,* New London fishermen, and his own crossing of the Grand Banks on the *New York* and *Philadelphia.*

There are more autobiographical references—in particular, O'Neill's American Line experience—as the characters discuss the Peasant Woman and other passengers on board their ship.

THE OTHER MAN: But you asked me if I had seen the woman. I don't think so because I never went down into the steerage. I know some of the first class passengers did but I wasn't curious. It's a filthy sort of hole, isn't it?

THE DARK MAN: It's not so bad. I spent quite a good deal of my time down there.

THE BUSINESS MAN: In your role of reformer?

THE DARK MAN: No. Simply because I found the people in the steerage more interesting to talk to than the second class passengers. I am not a reformer—at least not in the professional sense.

THE BUSINESS MAN: Do you mind my asking what particular line you are in?

THE DARK MAN: I am a writer (O'Neill, CP1, 102).

Through the Dark Man, revealed as the Poet, O'Neill exposes himself as a writer and expresses his comfort with working class people and his discomfort with people of his own class. O'Neill shows his distaste for first- and second-class passengers who had been aboard the American Line, illustrated by the Business Man's comment that some first-class passengers went down to steerage out of curiosity, as if the steerage passengers were an oddity. O'Neill would explore this idea further in *The Hairy Ape*.

O'Neill depicts himself further in the play when the Poet mentions his own suicidal tendencies. He tells the Business Man that when the ship was sinking he went below to steerage to hide so that he would die when the ship went down. But he found the Peasant Woman and her child and felt that he had to rescue them. In order to rescue them he had to save himself. The Business Man asks if he has given up on the idea of suicide. The Poet responds: "I have—absolutely. I think all that happened to me is an omen sent by the Gods to convince me my past unhappiness is past and my fortune will change for the better" (O'Neill, CP1, 104). In this optimistic statement, O'Neill is giving voice to the positive change in his life. His discharge from Gaylord is 18 months in the past, and he has begun to find his place in life and to discover the joy in writing.

THE GLENCAIRN PLAYS

Bound East for Cardiff (1914), *In the Zone* (1917), *The Long Voyage Home* (1917), and *The Moon of the Caribbees* (1917) are known as the Glencairn plays. They revolve around the experiences of the crew of the fictitious "SS *Glencairn*" and are drawn from O'Neill's time aboard the SS *Ikala*. In a letter to H. L. Mencken, dated 26 May 1917, regarding possible publication of *The Long Voyage Home* and *The Moon of the Caribbees,* O'Neill identified them as: "units in a series." "They deal with merchant-sailor life on a tramp steamer as it really is—its sordidness inexplicably touched with romance by the glamour of far horizons." Though each play was complete, characters reappeared "because, from my own experience as a sailor, I thought I had, in the majority of cases, picked out the typical mixed crew of the average British tramp."[42]

With these plays, O'Neill caught the attention of the literary and theatrical world. They launched his career.

In a prophetic statement, Jig Cook, a founder of the Provincetown Players, announced to a friend when she arrived in Provincetown:

> You don't know Gene yet. You don't know his plays. But you will. All the world will know Gene's plays some day. Last summer this thing [Provincetown Players] began. This year, on the night he first came to Provincetown and read us *Bound East for Cardiff,* we knew we had something to go with. Some day this little theater will be famous; some day the little theater in New York will be famous—this fall the Provincetown Players go into New York with *Cardiff* on their first bill (Sheaffer, SP, 358).

Bound East for Cardiff is a simple story about the relationship and adventures shared by two sailors. It comes directly from the life O'Neill had shared with sailors in Buenos Aires and aboard the *Ikala* and *Charles Racine.* In 1934 O'Neill corresponded with Richard Dana Skinner, who was working on a critical study of O'Neill's plays and wanted a list of when they had been written. O'Neill went into particular detail about *Bound East for Cardiff:*

> 1914 (Spring)—*Bound East for Cardiff* (Very important, this play! In it can be seen—or felt—the germ of the spirit, life-

attitude, etc. of all my significant future work—and it was written practically within my first half-year as a playwright, before I went to Baker [referring to the playwriting course at Harvard], under whose influence the following year I did nothing worth 1/10 as original. Remember in these U.S. in 1914 *Bound East for Cardiff* was a daring innovation in form and content).[43]

Originally, *Bound East for Cardiff* was called *Children of the Sea.* O'Neill revised and renamed the play during his first summer in Provincetown as he prepared it for its first production by the Provincetown Players. Most of the revisions to the script were minor. But he made one significant cut, a story that Driscoll told Yank about the apparent murder of a brutal mate at sea. That summer the production of *Bound East for Cardiff* was directed by O'Neill, and he took the minor role of the Second Mate. The Provincetown Players' props and sets for their productions had been impressionistic, but O'Neill insisted on realism in the production (Egan, 6). His script required a realistic approach because it dealt with the true emotions of ordinary working men.

In creating the play, O'Neill drew upon his memories of the bonds and relationships among sailors and in particular his friend Driscoll, who was the inspiration for both Driscoll and Yank in *Bound East for Cardiff.* As Yank lies dying in his bunk, he and Driscoll reminisce about their experiences. The segment that was cut from the original version has Driscoll telling Yank about being on a Yankee bark loaded with lumber bound from Nova Scotia to the River Plate. Conditions were poor and the captain and mate abusive. The crew tried to reason with the mate, but their complaints were ignored. Driscoll continues telling Yank:

> DRISCOLL: The rest av the story is best not told but I'll tell it to you. Wan dark rainy night off Rio the mate and the man at the wheel were alone on the poop—and the mate slipped and fell over the side. He was missing at the end av the watch.

> YANK: *(sarcastically)* Huh, slipped and fell over the rail, too, I suppose? The man at the wheel oughta made up a better lie than that. Did he say he seen him fall over?

> DRISCOLL: No.

Provincetown Players production of *Bound East for Cardiff* (Sheaffer-O'Neill Collection, Connecticut College)

YANK: Or heard a splash?

DRISCOLL: He saw nothin' and heard nothin'; but the mate must have slipped because he was nowhere to be found.

YANK: The guy at the wheel had his nerve with him. Who was he?

DRISCOLL: I was; and if I've nivir told ye before t'was because it's past and gone these fifteen years, and best forgotten.

YANK: *(after a pause)* He got what was coming to him—the mate, I mean.

DRISCOLL: He was a dirty dog; I have no regrets for him. The captain wint round wid a pisthol strapped about his waist in plain sight afther that, but the food was much betther (O'Neill, Children, 98).

Stephen Black suggests that O'Neill may have cut this story from the play because it was true, or at least O'Neill believed it to be true, as told to him by the real Driscoll.

O'Neill may well have based the story on the slave-driving "bucko" mate he experienced aboard the *Timandra*, when he worked loading hides in Buenos Aires. O'Neill sets Driscoll's story on a bark carrying lumber from Nova Scotia to Buenos Aires, a typical route for the *Charles Racine* and *Timandra*.

Yank and Driscoll also recall the memorable times they had together in Buenos Aires sleeping on park benches, going to the Sailor's Opera, and to the moving pictures in Barracas, as O'Neill himself had done. Driscoll complains about the quality of the food on board ship, and the men trade stories about shipwrecks and other disasters. Yank, reminiscing about Buenos Aires, says, "Remember the time we was there on the beach and had to go to Tommy Moore's boarding house to git shipped? And he sold us rotten oilskins and seaboots full of holes, and shipped us on a skys'l yarder round the Horn, and took two months' pay for it" (O'Neill, CP1, 196). Here, O'Neill gives an accurate picture of the process and the conditions for deep-water sailors. He had heard sailors recollect their shared experiences and adventures, and he was acquainted with unscrupulous men like Tommy Moore in Buenos Aires.

Yank refers to the "stink of the hides" in La Plate (O'Neill, CP1, 196), which is an echo of O'Neill's experience working at the Swift Packing House. As Yank is dying he tells Driscoll to take his pocket watch and that he and the other men should divide up his pay after he is gone, illustrating the generosity O'Neill had found among sailors. Typically, the effects of a dead seaman were auctioned off to the crew.

O'Neill expresses his knowledge of life aboard ship in different ways throughout the play, beyond the relationships among sailors. At the beginning of the play he sets the time: "It is nearing the end of the dog watch—about ten minutes to eight in the evening" (O'Neill, CP1, 187). Dogwatches are two short watches, or work periods, of two hours apiece. The first is from four o'clock in the afternoon to six o'clock; the second begins at six and ends at eight. Normal watches were four hours long. By creating an uneven number of watch periods through the day, dogwatches ensured that the men worked on a rotating schedule from day to day. Since the dogwatches were short, the men off watch by tradition used the time to socialize or do things for themselves.

O'Neill reveals his knowledge of medical care aboard ship. In the event a man is ill or injured, it is the responsibility of the captain to administer medical care. His knowledge depended on previous experience and a reference book. After examining Yank, the Captain says to Driscoll: "Keep him quiet and we'll hope for the best. I'll read up and send him some medicine, something to ease the pain, anyway" (O'Neill, CP1, 194).

Two more successes followed for O'Neill. In November of 1917, *In the Zone* was produced by the Washington Square Players, and the Provincetown Players opened their season with *The Long Voyage Home*. Both plays continued with the exploits of the crew of the "SS *Glencairn*." In a survey of the theater season in New York, the *Boston Transcript* published a lengthy discussion of the two plays and said of O'Neill, "Clearly here is an unusual talent for the observation of life and the manipulation of theatrical effect" (Sheaffer, SP, 393–94).

The Long Voyage Home sheds light on the sailor's life ashore and the dangers he encounters in sailortown. It is a classic story of a shanghaiing. Olson has decided to give up the sea and return home to his family farm in Sweden. He has just signed off the *"Glencairn"* and therefore has his pay. He and his shipmates go into one of the many sailors' bars. Olson insists that he will not drink anything but ginger beer, be watchful of his money, and not get drunk. He does not want to squander his savings and ruin his plans to return home. Through the conniving efforts of Joe (the bar owner), Freda (a prostitute), and Nick (whom O'Neill describes as a crimp), Olson is drugged and shipped out to sea against his will.

The inspiration for the character of Olson could have been any number of people in O'Neill's life. There are similarities between Chris Christopherson and Olson. Also, there was Gabrielsen, the first mate on the *Charles Racine,* who had been sending money home to his fiancée for 20 years (Sheaffer, SP, 166). Another was Hanson, the *Racine's* sailmaker. At one time, Hanson signed off the ship in Antwerp with two years' pay. He spent some in town and was robbed of the rest. He returned to the ship with hardly any clothes (Sheaffer, SP, 166). Each of these individuals, along with general sailors' longings and fantasies of returning home to the farm, contributed to O'Neill's idea for the character of Olson.

Through this story, O'Neill portrays the sailor's naiveté and inability to control his fate.

Prior to Olson and his shipmates entering into the action of the play, Joe and Nick have a conversation that introduces their shanghai plot. Through their runners they know that four "two-year men" (O'Neill, CP1, 510) have signed off the *"Glencairn"* and will be coming into the bar. "Two-year men" were sailors who had two years' pay in their pockets.

> NICK: Reason I arst yer about the drops was 'cause I seen the capt'n of the Amindra this arternoon.
>
> JOE: The Amindra? Wot ship is that?
>
> NICK: Bloody windjammer—skys'l yarder—full rigged—painted white—been layin' at the dock above 'ere fur a month. You knows 'er.
>
> JOE: Ho, yus. I knows now.
>
> NICK: The capt'n says as 'e wants a man special bad—ter-night. They sails at daybreak ter-morrer.
>
> JOE: There's plenty o' 'ands lyin' abaht waitin' fur ships, I should fink.
>
> NICK: Not fur this ship, ole buck. The capt'n an' mate are bloody slave-drivers, an' they're bound down round the 'Orn. They 'arf starved the 'ands on the larst trip 'ere, an' no one'll dare ship on 'er *(after a pause)* I promised the capt'n faithful I'd get 'im one, and ter-night (O'Neill, CP1, 511).

Nick, the crimp, wants knockout drops handy to slip into a sailor's drink to insure delivering a man as promised. The Gelbs suggest that Nick is modeled after Shanghai Brown, a crimp in Liverpool (Gelb, LWMC, 301). Shanghai Brown was a well-known name among sailors—there was even a fo'c's'le song by that name, which has an alternate title "Go To Sea No More." The lyrics tell of a man who was shanghaied by Brown for a whaling voyage in the Arctic, which would place Shanghai Brown in San Francisco. A second version of the song replaces the name "Shanghai Brown" with "Rapper Brown," who was a crimp in Liverpool (Hugill, SSS, 403–05). But "Shanghai Brown" can also be seen as the icon of all crimps, a folkloric figure like Paul Bunyan or Johnny Appleseed. Many men and women in O'Neill's experience could have been the prototype for Nick the Crimp, including Tommy Moore in Buenos Aires, as well as numerous other crimps from Buenos Aires, New York, and Southampton.

The fictional ship *"Amindra"* is drawn from O'Neill's experience with the *Timandra,* on which he worked briefly while it was in port in Buenos Aires. The ship's hard-case mate—"that old bucko of a first mate," who "would drop a marlin spike on your skull" (Sheaffer, SP, 177) was forever locked in his memory. The white-painted *Timandra* was about the same size as the *Charles Racine,* but it carried more sail than the *Racine* since it was a full-rigged ship (with square sails on all three masts) and the *Racine* was bark-rigged (with square sails on two masts and fore-and-aft sails on one).

O'Neill describes the *"Amindra"* as a "skys'l yarder" and "full-rigged." The ship of O'Neill's experience—the *Charles Racine*—was a bark, not a full-rigged ship and did not have skysails, but the *Timandra* was full-rigged and did carry a main skysail. A skysail is the sixth square sail in the sequence from bottom to top. A feature of much earlier clipper ships and other ships heavily rigged for speed, it had largely fallen out of use by the late 1800s. Later European-design ships had wider, lower rigs, five sails high—terminating with royals—but a few vessels still carried skysails above their royals. Being a "skys'l yarder" and "full-rigged" meant that the *"Amindra"* carried a large number of sails for its day, compounding the problem of finding enough sailors. The laws of the time stipulated that the crew size was determined roughly by the tonnage of the ship. For heavily rigged vessels, this formula for crew size was inadequate. To make matters worse, vessels were undermanned for economic reasons as well (Weibust, 40).

The other dramatically complicating factor is that the *"Amindra"* sailed around Cape Horn or "round the 'Orn," as Nick says. Rounding the Horn is one of the most difficult passages at sea, particularly sailing from the Atlantic into the Pacific, since the prevailing winds blow from west to east. Any sailor who knew his trade would have been aware of the potential of being worked to death aboard the *"Amindra."* The prospect of sailing on such a ship, with insufficient crew, would send fear into a sailor's heart.

Once Olson has entered into the action of the play and is slipped the knockout drops, one of the roughs lets the name *"Amindra"* drop. Upon hearing the name Olson says, "I know dat damn ship—worst ship dat sail to sea. Rotten grub and dey make you work all time—and the Captain and Mate wus Bluenose devils. No sailor know anything ever ship on her. Where iss she bound from here?" The rough responds, "Round Cape 'Orn—sails at daybreak." Olson continues; "Py yingo, I pity poor fallers make dat trip round Cape Stiff dis time year. I bet you some of dem never see port once again" (O'Neill, CP1, 521–22). Olson's words realistically depict how a sailor would react to serving on the *"Amindra."*

The third of the Glencairn plays, *The Moon of the Caribbees,* takes place aboard the *"Glencairn,"* anchored off an island in the West Indies. The sounds of life and activity ashore carry across the water to the ship. The men are close to shore, but not close enough. They are restless on deck as they await the arrival of the bumboat women with wares and "favors" to sell. The expectation of the women's arrival heightens the men's thirst for alcohol and female companionship. Tension increases with the crew knowing they will have to hide the rum and women from the officers, disguising their purchases of contraband and claiming they have only bought fruit and souvenirs.

The Moon of the Caribbees was one of O'Neill's personal favorites. He said it "was my first real break with theatrical tradition." He referred to it as the "pet of all my one-acters" (Sheaffer, SP 383). In a letter to Barrett Clark in 1919, O'Neill spoke of *The Moon of the Caribbees* as distinctly his: "The spirit of the sea—a big thing—is in this latter play, is the hero."[44]

The inspiration for *The Moon of the Caribbees* obviously draws on the time that the *Ikala* anchored off the island of Trinidad. O'Neill had originally titled the play "The Moon at Trinidad" (Sheaffer-O'Neill Collection). It was very common for ships coming up from the South American ports of Buenos Aires, Montevideo, or Rio de Janeiro to stop at the large Caribbean islands of Trinidad or Barbados, so the experience was not unique to O'Neill and the *Ikala.*

Within minutes of a ship's dropping anchor it would be swarming with groups of women and bumboat men, eager to sell cheap rum (Hugill, ST, 230–31). Bumboats were common in many ports and islands where ships anchored off rather than lying at wharves. They would come alongside the vessel, board, and spread their wares out on the deck. The bumboats could be major suppliers for ships who needed to replenish their provisions (Weibust, 154).

In *The Moon of the Caribbees* the character names of Lamps, the lamp-trimmer, and Chips, the carpenter, are drawn from O'Neill's knowledge of tramp steamers and the nicknames for certain seamen. O'Neill is very specific in his list of characters, ascribing to each their responsibilities. Others are simply listed as firemen or seamen of the tramp steamer *"Glencairn"* or West Indian negresses (O'Neill, CP1, 526). The specific information about Lamps and Chips does not enhance the action of the play in any way, but expresses O'Neill's intimate knowledge of the workings of ships.

In addition to details about the crew, O'Neill adds authenticity by playing on his knowledge of chanteys. In *The Moon of the Caribbees* the crew asks Driscoll to sing a chantey to drown out the tantalizing sounds coming from shore. They request "Rio Grande," "Whiskey Johnny," "Maid O'Amsterdam," and "Santa Anna" (O'Neill, CP1, 530). These were all well-known chanteys. "Whiskey Johnny" was sung at the halyard to coordinate the effort of raising the square sails. The other three chanteys were used at the windlass or capstan when raising the anchor or other heavy objects (Hugill, SSS, 43–80). O'Neill may have known that "Santa Anna" was a favorite chantey of the members of New London's Jibboom Club. The later three chanteys were more melodic since the work they accompanied generally took a long time.

In the play, Driscoll is a seaman and not a fireman as O'Neill's friend had been, and responds to the request for a chantey:

> Shut your mouths, all av you. *(scornfully)* A chanty is ut ye want? I'll bet me whole pay day there's not wan in the crowd 'ceptin Yank here, an Ollie, an' meself, an' Lamps an' Cocky, maybe, wud be sailors enough to know the main from the mizzen on a windjammer. Ye've herd the names av chanties but divil a note av the tune or a loine an the words do ye know. There's hardly a rale deep-water sailor lift on the seas, more's the pity (O'Neill, CP1, 530–31).

Driscoll comments on the fact that sailors no longer know the difference between the masts, questioning if there are any sailors left who had to sing a chantey to get the work done. Of course, such work songs had no place on a steamship, where coordinated physical effort was not required.

**1924 Provincetown Players production of *The Moon of the Caribbees*
(Sheaffer-O'Neill Collection, Connecticut College)**

In pointing out how archaic this tradition of the sea had become, O'Neill
mourns the end of the age of sail through the character of Driscoll.

The fourth Glencairn play is *In the Zone*. Although it was O'Neill's
least favorite of the four, it was his most commercially successful one-act
play (Sheaffer, SP, 383). While the other Glencairn plays are set earlier, it is
set during the First World War. The action of the play takes place in the
fo'c's'le of the munitions-carrying *"Glencairn."* The play revolves around
the tension that arises when a seaman is observed hiding something from
his fellow shipmates. There is already an atmosphere of suspicion and
anxiety rising out of the threat of being sunk by a German U-boat, so it is
not surprising that Smitty is suspected of being a spy. He is thought to be
hiding a bomb. O'Neill speaks to his own remembered feelings through
the character Ivan. "I don't li–ike dees voyage. Next time I ship on wind-

jammer Boston to River Plate, load with wood only so it float, by golly!" (O'Neill, CP1, 472).

In the 31 October 1917 edition of the *Boston Globe*, Louis Sherwin commented on the Washington Square Players production of *In the Zone*. "I don't know where this young man got his knowledge of the speech of seafaring men, but this is the second play he has written about them with remarkable power and penetration" (Sheaffer, SP, 393).

A number of personal experiences in O'Neill's past would have moved him in the writing of this script. Certainly his time at sea played its part, but there was another dramatic event from which he might have drawn. In the spring of 1917, O'Neill and his friend Harold DePolo were arrested in Provincetown on the suspicion of being spies. It was early in the season, and O'Neill and DePolo had been spending a great deal of time walking the beaches. The U.S. had just entered the war against Germany, and in the climate of war in that remote place, the people of Provincetown were wary of the activity of these two strangers and imagined they were searching the beaches for a possible landing site for an invasion. Rumors grew, with claims that O'Neill and DePolo had guns and a wireless. The fact that O'Neill sometimes carried his typewriter in its case on his walks helped fuel the rumors. They were arrested and put in jail while the Secret Service was summoned from Boston. After a night in jail, O'Neill was recognized as being James O'Neill's son and the two were released. Both DePolo and O'Neill later claimed that the play had already been written by this time (Sheaffer, SP, 393). But the coincidence of the arrest and the play raises the question.

The torpedoing of the transatlantic liner *Lusitania* by a German U-boat in May 1915 could also have been on O'Neill's mind when he wrote his play. With the escalation of war to noncombatant ships and the resulting deaths of approximately 760 passengers and 440 members of the crew, it was a signal maritime tragedy (Miller, 83). Having traveled the same route across the North Atlantic, O'Neill would have had some deep, shivering thoughts.

While O'Neill worked for the *New London Telegraph,* an article appeared on 19 September 1912, which might have contributed to his thoughts for *In the Zone.* The story was of an incident surrounding a small black box, which had been left for safekeeping with a shopkeeper. The shopkeeper became suspicious and notified the police. Everyone was alarmed at what might be inside. When the box was finally opened it contained nothing but a man's clothing (Sheaffer, SP, 381–82).

The possible sources of inspiration for *In the Zone* are unlimited, but underlying them all was O'Neill's personal knowledge of sailors' customs and etiquette. In speaking to the other seamen about Smitty's secretiveness Davis says: "He's been on ship near two year, ain't he? He knows damn well there ain't no thiefs in this fo'c's'le, don't he?" (O'Neill, CP1, 477). As mentioned earlier, trust was a linking force among shipmates. The confined conditions in which they lived, and the work they did, demanded it. Sailors had their own strict code of justice. If a sailor were found stealing from his shipmates, the punishments administered by his fellow sailors could be severe. But nothing could compare to being shunned by shipmates. It made a sailor's life miserable (Weibust, 193). O'Neill was fully aware of the climate of trust and honesty among sailors. Davis is so taken aback by Smitty's secretiveness that he begins to question if Smitty is a sailor at all.

The suspicion escalates to a point where the crew becomes hostile and attacks Smitty. Against his protests they open the box he has hidden and find letters. They are relieved that it does not contain a bomb, but their suspicion does not abate. They assume that he is a spy and the letters must contain secret information. As they read the letters they discover they are from the woman Smitty loves and that she has given up on him, calling him a drunk and accusing him of ruining her life. The play ends with all the shipmates in agony over their violent invasion into Smitty's personal life and feeling acutely his demoralization—a depth of emotion most sailors could recognize in their marginalized role in society.

THE PERSONAL EQUATION

O'Neill wrote *The Personal Equation*, originally called the "The Second Engineer," in the spring of 1915, while attending George Pierce Baker's playwriting course at Harvard. O'Neill was not happy with the play and destroyed all his copies—as he did with other drafted plays that did not satisfy him—so it was never copyrighted, produced, or published by O'Neill. A copy did survive, however, at the Houghton Library at Harvard.

The play's primary characters are Thomas Perkins, second engineer of the "SS *San Francisco*," his son Tom, and Tom's mistress Olga, an anarchist. The play has four acts, which take place in the headquarters of the International Workers Union in Hoboken, New Jersey, at the home of Thomas Perkins, aboard the *"San Francisco,"* and in a Liverpool hospital.

The play tells the story of the "International Workers Union's" intention to start a worldwide strike. In order to awaken the workers and instigate the strike, Tom agrees to blow up the engines of his father's ship when it arrives in Liverpool. The explosion will be the signal for the workers to rise up and seize power from the oppressive bosses and lead the workers to freedom. O'Neill is making a reference to the Industrial Workers of the World (I.W.W.), the revolutionary union established in 1905, which included dockworkers and which opposed the war. In order not to be discovered by his father, Tom disguises himself and signs on as a stoker for the steamer. As the steamer docks in Liverpool, war breaks out in Europe. Olga comes on board the ship, disguised as a man, to tell Tom that the workers, in a show of patriotism, have refused to back the I.W.U. The audience learns that Olga is pregnant with Tom's child—another personal resonance for O'Neill. Tom gains the support of the more radical members of the crew and they decide to wreck the ship's engines. The play reaches a climax when Tom is confronted in the engine room by his father. Thomas Perkins is forced to shoot his son in order to protect the engines. The final act takes place in a hospital room in Liverpool where Tom is a patient. He has severe brain damage from the gunshot. During the scene Olga and Perkins reconcile their differences and vow to devote their lives to the care of Tom.

O'Neill obviously drew from his experiences with the American Line and his time in Southampton during the Great General Strike of

1911. Early in the play Enwright, one of the members of the I.W.U., mentions that they are gathering together to discuss the planned strike by dockworkers, seamen, and firemen. The dockworkers were at the heart of the 1911 strike in England and were then joined by the seamen and firemen. The fictional *"San Francisco"* can be seen as the *New York* or *Philadelphia* on which O'Neill worked. The character of Tom also bears some resemblance to O'Neill, who is referring to his year at Princeton when Tom mentions that he had wasted one year at college. Later in the play there is another autobiographical reference when Tom mentions that he has made a round trip on an ocean steamer. Tom says that his job was as a stoker, although O'Neill had been a seaman. O'Neill expresses his own revelation from the American Line experience when Tom discusses that he never could have imaged the conditions on board a ship for the stokers and how they contrasted with the lifestyle of the first-class passengers.

An analogy can be drawn between O'Neill's home life and his relationship with his father and those of the character Tom. Tom's mother died when he was young, so she was lost to him during his early years. Due to her addiction, O'Neill's mother was almost equally absent during his childhood. Mr. Perkins bears a likeness to James O'Neill in that both men were dedicated to their work to such an extent that they were rarely in one place for very long and had no permanent home. Perkins is devoted to his ship and its engines. Tom mentions that when his father was transferred from an "old ship" to a new one Perkins cried because he hated leaving the "old engines." According to Tom, Perkins does not know anything but his engines and will speak about them for hours. Tom says that his father's "life is bound up in just that one thing—marine engines" (O'Neill, CP1, 318–19). Perkins's desire to remain with the "old ship" and "old engines" is mirrored in James O'Neill's commitment to the same theatrical vehicle, *The Count of Monte Cristo,* a choice that stifled his personal and professional growth, but one that was safe. James O'Neill eventually expressed some regret about his reliance on that one play but not until his later years. At the time that O'Neill wrote *The Personal Equation, The Count of Monte Cristo* was still James O'Neill's mainstay. Tom's statement that he was "lulled to sleep" with "twin-screw lullaby" is an allusion to O'Neill's own infancy and being on tour with his father.

The *Personal Equation* and *The Hairy Ape* share some similarities. Both of the plays have scenes that are set in the firemen's fo'c's'le and labor union headquarters. The stage directions for Act Three, Scene One, of *The Personal Equation,* which is set in the "fireman's fo'castle," are very similar to those of Scene One of *The Hairy Ape.* In *The Personal Equation* there is much greater detail, and Hogan sings the songs "Whiskey Johnny" and "Beer, Beer, Glorious Beer." These songs are also sung by Paddy in *The Hairy Ape.* Even though O'Neill did not like *The Personal Equation* as a whole, elements that met his approval would be incorporated into *The Hairy Ape* six years later.

ILE

O'Neill wrote *Ile*—New England dialect for oil—in Provincetown in 1917, and it was produced by the Provincetown Players that November. Captain John Cook and his wife Viola of Provincetown and their experiences in the Arctic, described earlier, inspired the play. *Ile* is set on a steam whaler in the Arctic Ocean. The ship is commanded by the fictional Captain David Keeney—whom O'Neill christened with the name of an actual New London whaling family—who is obsessed with the hunt for whales so he can have a profitable voyage. Against the wishes of his wife and mutinous crew, he pushes further north in pursuit of whales. His wife is driven crazy from her long period in the Arctic, longing for home, and from witnessing the brutality of her husband.

As with *The Personal Equation,* O'Neill explored his own family's relationships through the characters in *Ile.* In this case it was the relationship between his mother and father. As a whaling captain, David Keeney was required to travel almost all the time, with the occasional season at home, which is analogous to James O'Neill's career as an actor. Both Keeney and James O'Neill were in search of financial success; for Keeney that meant hunting whales in distant oceans and for James O'Neill it constituted relentless theatrical performances in towns across the country. Their wives were forced to confront the dilemma of accompanying their husbands or staying at home alone. It was a highly emotional decision, with women having to weigh their options and responsibilities, knowing that whatever they chose, each had its own form of loneliness. Like Viola Cook and the fictional Mrs. Keeney, Ella O'Neill was devoted to her husband and could not bear to be separated from him.

Ile was O'Neill's earliest attempt at exploring his parents' relationship. He would return to them in *Long Day's Journey into Night* in 1940. There are clear similarities between the married couples in the two plays: David and Annie Keeney of *Ile* and James and Mary Tyrone in *Long Day's Journey into Night*. Mrs. Keeney and Mary Tyrone are both removed from reality, but in different ways. Mrs. Keeney goes insane while Mary Tyrone's escape from reality is drug-induced. Each woman holds a romantic view of her husband and his career. Mary Tyrone sees her actor-husband as the dashing leading man who can command the stage. Mrs. Keeney's view of her husband is no less romantic: "I guess I was dreaming about the old Vikings in the story books and I thought you were one of them" (O'Neill, CP1, 500).

In *Ile*, Captain and Mrs. Keeney's relationship reflects that of O'Neill's parents. It is not an accurate reflection of many whaling families, and of John and Viola Cook specifically. Mrs. Keeney's frail constitution more closely resembles Ella O'Neill's than it does Viola Cook's. Captain and Mrs. Keeney have a lengthy discussion about her being with him on the voyage:

KEENEY: Remember, I warn't hankerin' to have you come on this voyage, Annie.

MRS. KEENEY: I wanted to be with you, David, don't you see? I didn't want to wait back there in the house all alone as I've been doing these last six years since we were married—waiting, and watching, and fearing—with nothing to keep my mind occupied—not able to go back teaching school on account of being Dave Keeney's wife. I used to dream of sailing on the great, wide, glorious ocean. I wanted to be at your side in the danger and vigorous life of it all. I wanted to see you the hero they make you out to be in Homeport. And instead—(*Her voice grows tremulous.*) All I find is ice and cold—and brutality! (*Her voice breaks.*)

KEENEY: Oh, I warned ya what it'd be, Annie. "Whalin' ain't no ladies' tea party," I says to you, and "you better stay home where you've got your woman's comforts." (*Shaking his head*) But you was so set on it (O'Neill, CP1, 500).

O'Neill's depiction of the wife waiting at home for her husband to return from the sea with nothing to do is the cliché of the New England sea captain's wife standing on the widow's walk atop her home staring out to sea. Mrs. Cook joined her husband on a number of voyages. Some women certainly did not choose to accompany their husbands, while others decided after one trip that they would never go again. Many women, however, along with their children, went on numerous voyages and gave birth to children at sea. For those who chose to stay behind, in many maritime communities it was common for women to work while their husbands were gone, a necessity to support the family until the husband returned.[45]

O'Neill either did not understand the dynamics of whaling families or else he adapted the story to meet the dramatic needs of the play. But, at the same time, many elements of the play are faithful to the Cooks' experiences and life on a steam whaler in the Arctic. *Ile* takes place on a single day in 1895. It is the day the crew's term of service is to end. In earlier days of whaling, generally when a crew signed on the termination date was open-ended. It was up to the captain to release the crew when they were no longer needed—normally at the end of the voyage. During the period in which *Ile* is set, sailors had acquired greater rights and the custom was to sign on for a specific length of time. The crew of the *"Atlantic Queen,"* the fictional ship in *Ile*, has signed on for a two-year voyage. Captain Cook had his crew sign on for a three-year voyage. He intended to be out for approximately 20 months, but he had his crew sign on for a longer period should he decide to extend the trip. In the end, Cook's voyage lasted 44 months. At the outset of the play the Steward and Ben, the cabin boy, discuss the situation—the positions of cabin boy and steward are paid crew, but they associate with the officers, giving them the opportunity to explain things as a Greek chorus would.

> BEN: *(going over to him—in a half whisper)* They said if he don't put back south for home to-day they're going to mutiny.
>
> STEWARD: *(with grim satisfaction)* Mutiny? Aye, 'tis the only thing they can do; and serve him right after the manner he's treated them—'s if they wern't no better nor dogs.
>
> BEN: The ice is all broke up to the s'uth'ard. They's clear water 's far 's you can see. He ain't got no excuse for not turnin' back for home, the men says (O'Neill, CP1, 493).

A few moments later in the play the Mate says to Captain Keeney: "I'm afeard there'll be trouble with the hands by the look o' things. They'll likely turn ugly, every blessed one o' them, if you don't put back. The two years they signed up for is up to-day" (O'Neill, CP1, 495).

In O'Neill's play, the action that ensues is consistent with Cook's account, except O'Neill exaggerates the events and condenses them to occur in one day to heighten the dramatic tension. O'Neill's portrayal of the confrontation is an accurate depiction within the seafaring context. The Mate warns Captain Keeney that the crew might take him to court when they return home, which is what Captain Cook's crew did. Cook had to pay a fine, which he claimed was unjust, arguing that if he had been able to be in the courtroom the ruling would have turned out differently. The suit went before a court in San Francisco, which was the base for Arctic whaling, and Cook was in Provincetown at the time.

Captain Keeney says to the Mate: "What do the fools want to go home fur now? Their share o' the four hundred barrel wouldn't keep 'em in chewin' terbacco" (O'Neill, CP1, 497). Keeney is saying that the voyage has not been profitable yet, and if they turn for home no one will have earnings of any significance, since the crew's pay is based on a share of the profits. The 400 barrels refers to barrels of whale oil. It is important to point out that during this period Arctic whalers were primarily seeking baleen from whales, which had significant value, whereas the oil was secondary. It does not appear that O'Neill was familiar with this aspect of whaling and perhaps was thinking of an earlier period, such as the heyday of New London whaling, when oil was the primary product. Or perhaps, O'Neill knew that the public was not familiar with whaling, and Arctic whaling would have been too complicated to explain in the context of his play.

Even though there are some inaccuracies in the play regarding Arctic whaling, O'Neill demonstrates his knowledge about life on board a ship. For example, the opening dialogue of the play is between the Steward and Ben, the cabin boy. The Steward is chastising Ben for going up to the fo'c's'le and being with the crew. The Steward warns Ben that if he is caught by the captain he will be punished. O'Neill illustrates his knowledge of the dividing line on board a ship and that the crew does not come aft unless there is work to be done and the officers and members of the "cabin staff" do not go forward. A cabin boy's responsibilities are to serve the captain and officers and he should not fraternize with the crew, though he is one of them by rank and pay.

Just as the name Keeney connotes whaling, the name that O'Neill gives the second mate—Slocum—connotes sailing. O'Neill may be paying homage to Joshua Slocum, who was the first man in recorded history to sail around the world alone. Slocum began his three-year adventure in 1895, the same year in which *Ile* is set. In 1899 Slocum wrote of his voyage in *Sailing Alone Around the World,* which became a classic of sea literature. It is more than likely, with his interest in the sea, that O'Neill read Slocum's book.

With *Ile,* O'Neill began to explore the relationship between his parents that he would examine in greater depth more than 20 years later in *Long Day's Journey into Night.* In this first examination of the subject, he sets it in the context of the sea, with which he has become so familiar. When it was first produced in 1917, *Ile* was regarded as one of the best American one-act plays ever written.

"TOMORROW"

O'Neill's only short story to be published was "Tomorrow," which appeared in *Seven Arts* magazine in June 1917. It is a first-person narrative set in a sailors' bar and flophouse in New York. O'Neill gave the narrator the name Art, which is likely drawn from his good friend Art McGinley of New London. "It was back in my sailor days, in the winter of my great down-and-outness, that all this happened," the story begins.

> In those years of wandering, to be broke and "on the beach" in some seaport or other of the world was no new experience; but this had been an unusually long period of inaction even for me. Six months before I had landed in New York after a voyage to Buenos Aires as able seaman on a British tramp. Since that time I had loafed around the water front eking out an existence on a small allowance from my family too lazy of body and mind, too indifferent to things in general, to ship to sea again or do anything else. I shared a small rear room with another "gentleman-ranker," Jimmy Anderson, an old friend of mine, over an all-night dive near South Street known as Tommy the Priest's (O'Neill, CP3, 947).

Clearly, O'Neill based the story on his own experiences, substituting the name Tommy the Priest's for the real Jimmy the Priest's.

Art goes on to say that the story is about his roommate Jimmy, a down-and-out Englishman of noble birth who had covered the Boer War as a reporter. Jimmy is based on O'Neill's friend Smitty, his roommate in Buenos Aires. The story is filled with events and individuals from O'Neill's days at sea and the sailortowns he visited. Driscoll appears as the character Lyons. Art says:

> Our door was kicked open with a bang and Lyons, the stoker, and Paddy Mehan, the old deepwater sailor, came crowding into the room. . . . They had been paid off that afternoon after a trip across on the American liner St. Paul (O'Neill, CP3, 957).

O'Neill's choice of the *"St. Paul"* is likely inspired by the real *St. Louis,* which was Driscoll's last ship, the one he jumped from to commit suicide. The actual *St. Paul* and the *St. Louis* were sister ships in transatlantic service, and Driscoll may have served on both. O'Neill recalls how he and Driscoll met for the first time when Art says:

> I had made a trip as a sailor on the Philadelphia when he [Lyons] was in her stokehold, and we had become great friends through a chance adventure together ashore in Southampton—which is another story (O'Neill, CP3, 957).

As the story unfolds it is clear that O'Neill is experimenting with characters and stories that he will later give voice to in a variety of his plays. Jimmy is seen again as Jimmy Tomorrow in *The Iceman Cometh,* and Paddy is a prominent figure in *The Hairy Ape.* In the short story, Paddy in his drunkenness sings two chanteys, including "Whiskey Johnny," which is sung in a number of O'Neill's plays. Lyons grabs Paddy and says: "That's the throuble wid all thim lazy, deck-scrubbers the loike av 'im" (O'Neill, CP3, 958). This exchange between the characters is an expression of the animosity that existed between stokers and seamen, a friction that O'Neill would illustrate in greater depth in *The Hairy Ape.*

O'Neill wrote "Tomorrow" in 1916, the same season that *Bound East for Cardiff* and *Thirst* received their first performances in Provincetown. The plays were successful, and it only seems natural that the young writer would continue to explore the maritime world that inspired his previous work. The short story can be seen as an exercise for O'Neill to begin to explore and reacquaint himself with the men he knew at Jimmy the Priest's. In the short story one can see the beginnings of a number of O'Neill's most important plays.

BEYOND THE HORIZON

O'Neill finished writing *Beyond the Horizon*, in 1918, when he was living in Provincetown. The play is set on a New England farm overlooking the sea. John D. Williams, a Broadway producer who was willing to take risks, paid O'Neill a $500 advance and placed the play under option. Years later Williams recalled:

> I had been trying to get Conrad to do a play for me. His sto-ries of the sea are so marvelous, but he simply cannot write a play. I wanted something with a feeling of the sea, without the sea scenes. . . . In *Beyond the Horizon* the farm is played against the sea, and is against the adventuring spirit of the latter. It is the most honest tragedy I have ever seen. . . . It is utterly devoid of "stage English," and is the only play by an American author I have ever seen which is (Sheaffer, SP, 422).

Beyond the Horizon opened on Broadway in February 1920. At first it was only presented at special matinees, sharing a theater with another play. But it immediately received critical acclaim and, once a Broadway the-ater became available, it moved to a new house for its own run. Alexander Woollcott of the *New York Times* said the play was "an absorb-ing, significant, and memorable tragedy, so full of meat that it makes most of the remaining fare seem like the merest meringue" (Gelbs, LWMC, 639). In recognition of the play O'Neill was awarded his first Pulitzer Prize that June.

The play is based on the familiar lament among sailors, wishing they had never left the family farm, and of succumbing to the lure of the sea and faraway places. O'Neill addresses these regrets in a number of his plays, including *The Long Voyage Home* and *Chris Christophersen*. O'Neill had known at least one sailor who cursed the day he left his family farm, a Norwegian sailor he met on the *Charles Racine,* who was the inspiration for Olsen in *The Long Voyage Home.*

The play revolves around two brothers, Andrew and Robert Mayo. At the opening of the play Robert, the younger brother, is preparing to go to sea with his uncle, Dick Scott, captain of the bark *"Sunda."* Robert has always wanted to leave the farm and see the world. On the other hand, Andrew has been content on the family farm and hopes to marry Ruth Atkins from a neighboring farm and settle down.

In the opening scene Ruth and Robert discover that they have been in love with each other and Robert, whose lifelong dream it has been, decides not to go to sea. When Andrew learns of this, he feels his future on the farm has been destroyed and chooses to leave and go to sea with his uncle. The tragedy of the play is that each of the brothers would have been better suited to their original goals and ambitions.

The character names are relevant to O'Neill's own life and interests. Mayo and Atkins are common family names in Provincetown and were the names of two members of the Peaked Hill Bars Life-Saving Station crew who drowned during a surfboat rescue mission in 1880. Even though O'Neill did not arrive in Provincetown until many years later, the memory of Mayo's and Atkins's heroism lived on. Through Captain Dick Scott, O'Neill pays homage to someone from his own youth. Captain T. A. Scott was a significant maritime figure in New London and grandfather of Maibelle Scott, O'Neill's girlfriend for a time.

O'Neill dipped into his own family and loosely modeled the characters of Andrew and Robert on his brother Jamie and himself. At the opening of the play, O'Neill describes Robert as "a tall, slender young man of twenty-three. There is a touch of the poet about him expressed in his high forehead and wide, dark eyes" (O'Neill, CP1, 573). Robert is the same age as the autobiographical character Edmund in *Long Day's Journey into Night.* Through Robert, O'Neill articulates some of the feelings and ideas that he will explore more fully in *Long Day's Journey into Night.* While speaking to Andrew, Robert expresses the same idealistic and poetic views as Edmund in *Long Days Journey into Night.* Robert says:

> Supposing I was to tell you that it's just Beauty that's calling
> me, the beauty of the far off and unknown, the mystery and
> spell of the East which lures me in the books I've read, the

need of the freedom of great wide spaces, the joy of wander-
ing on and on—in quest of the secret which is hidden over
there, beyond the horizon? Suppose I told you that was the
one and only reason for my going? (O'Neill, CP1, 577).

Edmund will convey similar views when he recalls his experiences at sea
while talking with his father.

In *Beyond the Horizon,* Andrew responds to his brother's longing for
beauty by saying:

Then you might as well stay here, because we've got all
you're looking for right on this farm. There's wide space
enough, Lord knows; and you can have all the sea you want
by walking a mile down to the beach; there's plenty of horizon to look at, and beauty enough for anyone, except in the
winter (O'Neill, CP1, 577).

Andrew's description is reminiscent of the New London and Provincetown areas that overlooked the sea, but might look desolate in winter, as
O'Neill knew well.

When Andrew returns to the farm he shares some of his sea adventures with his brother, a direct draw on O'Neill's experiences aboard the
Charles Racine riding out the hurricane and spending time in Buenos
Aires. Instead of a hurricane in the South Atlantic, O'Neill has Andrew
encounter a typhoon in the China Sea. Andrew says:

Had to run before it under bare poles for two days. I thought
we were bound down for Davy Jones, sure. Never dreamed
waves could get so big or wind blow so hard. If it hadn't been
for Uncle Dick being such a good skipper we'd have gone
down to the sharks, all of us. As it was we came out minus a
main top-mast and had to beat back to Hong-Kong for
repairs (O'Neill, CP1, 619–20).

Andrew tells his brother about some of the ports he visited.

Yes Sydney's a good town. *(enthusiastically)* But Buenos Aires
—there's the place for you. Argentine's a country where a
fellow has a chance to make good. You're right I like it. And
I'll tell you, Rob, that's right where I'm going just as soon as
I've seen you folks a while and can get a ship. I can get a berth

as second officer, and I'll jump the ship when I get there (O'Neill, CP1, 620–21).

Even though O'Neill did not experience the prosperity in Buenos Aires that Andrew expects, he had fond memories of the port city.

When O'Neill wrote *Beyond the Horizon* he was living at Peaked Hill Bars and did not have to choose between the lure of the sea or the land. He had the best of both worlds—the open ocean in front and solid earth behind. But he valued the memories and experiences from his vagabond days.

THE ROPE, WHERE THE CROSS IS MADE, AND GOLD

After completing *Beyond the Horizon,* O'Neill wrote four one-act plays, including *The Rope* and *Where the Cross Is Made.* Both *The Rope* and *Where the Cross Is Made* focus on the idea of hidden riches. *The Rope* was written in early 1918 and was produced by the Provincetown Players that April. It was published along with The Glencairn plays, *Ile,* and *Where the Cross Is Made* in a single volume titled *Seven Plays of the Sea.*

Of the seven plays, *The Rope* has the least connection with the sea. It takes place on the farm of Abraham Bentley, who lives there with his daughter Annie, her husband Sweeney, and their child Mary. Annie and her husband have barely enough money to pay the mortgage and provide for the family, and they are angry when they learn that in his will Bentley has left the farm to his prodigal son, Luke. A child of his second marriage, Luke left for the sea and has not been seen in five years. Annie and Sweeney also discover that when Bentley mortgaged the property he received the money in gold coins and hid them.

When Luke returns he has no interest in the farm or staying for any length of time. He says: "back after five years of bummin' round the rotten old earth in ships and things. Paid off a week ago—had a bust-up—and then took a notion to come out here—bummed my way—and here I am" (O'Neill, CP1, 557). His carefree attitude grates on the hard-working Annie and Sweeney. Luke, unintentionally, intensifies their contempt for his lightheartedness when he teaches his young niece Mary how to skip a coin on the sea, with the only coin he has. O'Neill is recalling his vagabond days and the other wanderers he had met during that time. Luke says to Sweeney:

> I don't want no truck with this rotten farm. You kin have my share of that. I ain't made to be no damned dirt puncher—not me! I ain't goin' to loaf around here more'n I got to, and when I goes this time I ain't never comin' back. Not me! Not to punch dirt and milk cows. You kin have the rotten farm for all of me. What I wants is cash—regular coin yuh kin spend—not dirt. I want to show the gang a real time, and then ship away to sea agen or go bummin' agen. I want coin yuh kin throw away—same's your kid chucked that dollar of mine overboard, remember? (O'Neill, CP1, 567).

Bentley sets in motion the irony of the play when he hangs a noose in the barn and says that Luke should hang himself when he returns home. No one challenges the father nor does anyone take the noose down. At the end of the play Mary climbs on a chair and grabs hold of the noose to swing from it. The rope comes away from the beam and a bag of gold coins topples down. Mary is ecstatic and one by one skips the coins into the sea.

The one-act play *Where the Cross Is Made* has a stronger connection with the sea. It is the story of a captain with the murder of two of his crew on his conscience, and his obsession with buried treasure.

Gold is a full-length version of the same story. O'Neill wrote *Where the Cross Is Made* in Provincetown in 1918, the first year he was there with Agnes. He had already outlined a full-length version, which later would become *Gold,* but the Provincetown Players wanted an O'Neill play to include in the opening of their 1918-19 season in New York. So O'Neill wrote *Where the Cross Is Made,* based on the third act of the outlined play. He completed *Gold* in 1920 while at Peaked Hill Bars. *Gold* opened on Broadway in June of the following year and closed after 13 performances.

In both of the plays O'Neill drew upon the knowledge of whaling he had acquired in New London and from the people he met in Provincetown, quite possibly from Captain Cook himself. This is not the Arctic whaling that is associated with *Ile,* but whaling in the tropics. The main character of the plays is Captain Isaiah Bartlett, who comes from a family of whaling captains. The action of *Where the Cross Is Made* takes place in Captain Bartlett's home on the coast of California. His son, Nat, recounts his father's experiences to Dr. Higgins, telling the doctor that Captain Bartlett returned from his last voyage seven years ago. He had expected the voyage to last two years, but he did not return for four years. During the voyage his ship was wrecked in the Indian Ocean. After seven days in an open boat the captain and six others managed to reach a small deserted island. When they were rescued from the island by a fleet of Malay canoes, only the captain and three others were alive: the mate Silas Horne, the bo'sun Cates, and Hawai'ian harpooner Jimmy Kanaka. They were "mad with thirst and starvation" when they were found. The four men finally made it to San Francisco and then home. While on the island the men had discovered what they believed to be treasure, and after returning home Bartlett sent his three companions back to the island on the schooner *"Mary Allen"* to retrieve the treasure. The *"Mary Allen"* was named after Bartlett's deceased wife. Bartlett kept a lookout for the *"Mary Allen"* for years even though he had been told that that the vessel had been wrecked and lost. Nat finishes telling the story to the doctor, who has come to evaluate Bartlett and will likely take him to the asylum.

At the end of the play the *"Mary Allen"* and its crew appear as ghosts, only seen by Bartlett and his son Nat. Bartlett welcomes his compatriots into the room. Silas Horn, Cates, and Jimmy Kanaka enter carrying chests of treasure. Bartlett's daughter, Sue, tries to calm her father and brother because she does not see what they see. Bartlett and his crew ascend the companionway to his rooftop lookout and slam the hatch behind them. Nat tries to follow but cannot open the door. Sue attempts to calm her brother. When the doctor arrives the ghostly nature of the scene disappears. The doctor is able to open the hatch and they find that Bartlett has died from heart failure. Nat finds a treasure map in his father's hand, and the play ends with the suggestion that Nat will follow in his father's footsteps, obsessed with retrieving the treasure that may or may not exist.

Sheaffer pointed out the similarity in the name of the schooner, *"Mary Allen"* in *Where the Cross Is Made*, and O'Neill's mother's first name, Mary Ellen. The fact that Bartlett is waiting for the *"Mary Allen"* to return from sea may be seen to symbolize James, Jamie, and Eugene's hope that Mrs. O'Neill would return from the depths of her morphine addiction (Sheaffer, SP, 430). By the time O'Neill was writing the play, Ella had been off morphine for a few years, but her drug-induced absence from his life in his youth still haunted him.

Gold is a more complex telling of the story from *Where the Cross Is Made* and deals with some of the events that lead up to the action in the earlier one-act play. The contagion of Bartlett's obsession over the treasure is developed further in the play, as Nat is drawn in. *Gold* has four acts and four additional characters: Butler and Abel, the cook and ship's boy, respectively, from Bartlett's wrecked ship; Sarah Allen, Bartlett's wife (O'Neill changed the name of the wife from the one used for the deceased wife in the one-act); and Daniel Drew, Sue Bartlett's fiancé, an officer on a freight steamer.

The first act is set on the deserted island, where Bartlett and his crew discover the supposed treasure, and it lays the foundation for the action in the rest of the play. The remaining three acts take place at Bartlett's home on the coast of California. In Act One, Butler claims that the treasure they have found is worthless copper and brass, not gold. Bartlett and the others grow suspicious of Butler and Abel and assume that they are trying to get the treasure for themselves. When a schooner is spotted that might mean their rescue from the island, Bartlett and his comrades decide to bury their treasure. They become concerned that Butler and Abel will tell the schooner captain, or that they will come back to dig up the treasure. Horne, Cates, and Jimmy suggest that they kill the other two. Bartlett says that killing them is against the law. Jimmy insists, saying that he can kill them. Bartlett does not respond verbally, but gives Jimmy an encouraging look. Jimmy interprets the look as a direct command and murders Butler and Abel. Bartlett absolves himself of any blame because he "spoke no word," but over time his guilt haunts him.

For the character of Jimmy Kanaka, O'Neill could be drawing on his New London whaling knowledge, since New London had links with the Hawai'ian Islands and many of the whalers from New England stopped in the islands to reprovision and sign on crew. Kanaka—Hawai'ian for people—was used by New England mariners as a generic term for people from the Hawai'ian Islands, or more broadly for Polynesians. Unable to pronounce their names, New England sailors gave islanders Christian first names, adding Kanaka as their surname.

Besides demonstrating his knowledge of whaling, in Act One of *Gold,* O'Neill again addresses a common theme among sailors of wanting to give up the sea and to return home. Once they have discovered the treasure, Bartlett says to Cates and Horne:

> Rum and wine for you three, and rest for me. Aye, I'll rest to home 'til the day I die. Aye, woman, I be comin' home now. Aye, Nat and Sue, your father be comin' home for the rest o' his life! I'll give up whalin' like ye've always been askin' me, Sarah. Aye, I'll go to meetin' with ye on a Sunday like ye've always prayed I would. We'll make the damn neighbors open their eyes, curse 'em! Carriages and silks for ye—they'll be nothin' too good—and for Sue and the boy. I've been dreamin' o' this for years. I never give a damn 'bout the oil— that's just trade—but I always hoped on some voyage I'd pick up ambergris—a whole lot of it—and that's worth gold! (O'Neill, CP1, 898).

O'Neill could be drawing on his knowledge of Captain Cook's successes, or whaling in general, when Bartletts' mentions his hope of finding ambergris and the money to be made from it because of its value. As discussed earlier, Captain Cook returned from his last whaling voyage in 1917, during which he found a significant amount of ambergris. Not long after Cook's return, O'Neill outlined *Gold.*

It is interesting that O'Neill has set the play on the coast of California. Since Bartlett is a whaling captain, and his father was one as well, it would be more typical for the play to have been set in New England. Whalers traveled the globe in search of whales, and during most of the whaling period the center of American whaling and the home ports for the ships were in New England. New England was also the distribution point for whale products, which in the early years of whaling were primarily derived from oil. Due to Arctic whaling, San Francisco became the principal whaling port from the 1880s to 1906 and developed a center for the manufacture of whale products—baleen and refined oil. Many New England captains moved to the West Coast to take advantage of the opportunities. O'Neill's setting suggests he was aware of the shift in American whaling from New England to San Francisco.

There is an obvious connection between *The Count of Monte Cristo* and *The Rope, Where the Cross Is Made,* and *Gold,* with the focus on hidden wealth and the discovery of buried treasure. In *The Count of Monte Cristo,* Edmund Dantes follows a treasure map that enables him to enact his revenge on those who imprisoned him. O'Neill would have seen many performances of this play when he accompanied his father on tour, until the swashbuckling plot became deeply embedded in his memory.

There is another story from O'Neill's New London years regarding buried treasure. In her 1916 book on New England seaports, Hildegarde Hawthorne recounted a New London incident about a Spanish galleon of the colonial period that was filled with gold and ran aground in New London during a storm. The gold was off-loaded for safekeeping, but when the Spaniards arrived with a new ship the gold was gone. It never resurfaced, and for many years it was believed that it was buried somewhere in New London (Hawthorne, 281–83). In *Gold,* O'Neill might have been combining *The Count of Monte Cristo* and the story of the Spanish galleon when Bartlett says:

> Years ago, when I was whalin' out o' New Bedford, a man come to me—Spanish-looking, he was—and wanted to charter my ship and me go shares. He showed me a map o' some island off the coast of South America somewhere. They was a cross marked on it where treasure had been buried by the old pirates. But I was a fool. I didn't believe him. He got old Scott's schooner finally. She sailed and never was heard o' since (O'Neill, CP1, 899).

CHRIS CHRISTOPHERSEN
AND "ANNA CHRISTIE"

Chris Christophersen, written in 1919, is O'Neill's first full-length play set entirely in the maritime context. The title character is based on O'Neill's friend Chris Christopherson from his days at Jimmy the Priest's. Christopherson also bears a resemblance to Olson in the Glencairn plays.

Both of the plays have autobiographical elements, but *Chris Christophersen* more so than *"Anna Christie."* O'Neill drew upon his experiences aboard the *Charles Racine* and the *Ikala* as well as his time at Jimmy the Priest's and in Provincetown, where he lived while writing the play. He changed the name of Jimmy's to Johnny the Priest's, and in the opening stage directions he offered a detailed and precise description of the establishment.

> Johnny "the Priest's" bar near South Street, New York City. On the left, forward, a large window looking out on the street. Beyond it, the main entrance, a double swinging door. Further back, another window. The bar runs from left to right nearly the whole length of the rear wall. In back of the bar, a small show case displaying a few bottles of case goods, for which there is evidently little call. The remainder of the rear space in front of the large mirrors is occupied by half-barrels of cheap whiskey of the nickel-a-shot variety, from which the liquor is drawn by means of brass spigots. On the right is an open doorway leading to the back room. Down front, at center and right of center, are two round, wooden tables with five chairs grouped about each (O'Neill, CP1, 797).

In stage directions for each scene of *Chris Christophersen,* O'Neill gives an accurate depiction of the locale, be it the deck of the barge or the fo'c's'le of the steamer *"Londonderry."* The opening description for Act Three, Scene One is extremely detailed, giving aspects of the layout and design of the fo'c's'le with one wall curved along the line of the ship's hull. The stage directions for the first scene declare, "It is late afternoon of a day in the fall of the year 1910 (O'Neill, CP1, 797)," which is prior to when O'Neill himself actually lived at Jimmy's.

Agnes Boulton wrote that the character of Anna appeared aloof and rather uninteresting. But she felt differently about the other characters:

> Old Chris—how real *he* was! It was Chris that Gene really knew and loved, and old Marthy too—and the bums and outcasts in the first act down at Johnny the Priest's saloon . . . in lower New York; the longshoremen, even the mailman— they all came to life (Boulton, 279).

The action of the play, in addition to being at Johnny the Priest's, takes place on board a coal barge at anchor in New York and en route to Boston, and on a steam freighter en route to, and at anchor in, Buenos Aires. All the locations of the ships and their routes are drawn from O'Neill's own experience.

In the opening, Larry (the bartender), and Johnny (the owner), are talking about Chris. Larry comments that being on a barge must be a terrible job. Johnny responds:

> Captain, mate, cook and crew! Seems to suit Chris alright. He's been at it a long time. Used to be a regular, deep-sea sailor years ago when he first got to comin' here—bo'sun on sailing ships. A good one on a windjammer, too, I guess. All them squareheads is good sailors (O'Neill, CP1, 800).

In his reference to "squareheads"—Scandinavians, or especially Norwegians —being good sailors, O'Neill is paying homage to Captain Waage and the crew of the *Charles Racine*.

Later in the first scene Mickey, an old shipmate of Chris's, comes in and they banter about the older days of sail. The scene vividly depicts the style of conversation at a place like Jimmy the Priest's. Chris says to Mickey:

> Ole *Neptune*. She vas mighty smart ship, dat one. Ay vas bo'-sun board of her tree year. Ain't no more fine ships like her on sea no more, py golly. *(He spits disgustedly.)* All is steamers now—damn tea-kettles. Dey ain't ships (O'Neill, CP1, 809).

Through Chris, O'Neill laments that the days of sail have gone, an expression of his own feelings and echoes of the feelings of the real Chris Christopherson and Captain Waage. O'Neill's use of the name *"Neptune"* could be drawn from the *Ikala*, whose original name was *Planet Neptune* when she was launched in 1901, but changed to *Ikala* with new ownership in 1909. It is likely that, when O'Neill was on board the *Ikala* in 1911, a good portion of the ship's equipment still bore the original name.

Even though the possible inspiration for the name was a steamer, and not a sailing vessel, O'Neill perhaps drew on some pleasant memories and superimposed them onto a sailing vessel for the reference here. Through Mickey, O'Neill gives a contrasting view of the *Ikala* experience. After an invitation from Chris to join him in his celebration of the imminent arrival of his daughter, Mickey says: "We're on the bust ourselves after a vige down to the Plate and back. We was paid off this morning—a stinkin', starvation, lime-juice tramp" (O'Neill, CP1, 809). Mickey is telling Chris that he and another sailor are celebrating after their trip to Buenos Aires and back on a British tramp steamer—like the *Ikala*—under less than adequate conditions, limey or lime-juice being a generalized maritime reference to the British Royal Navy's eighteenth- and nineteenth-century use of lime juice to prevent scurvy on board ship.

O'Neill expresses his personal views through a number of characters in the play, particularly Chris's daughter Anna and her love interest Paul Andersen. The Anna of the play *Chris Christophersen* differs from the Anna of the play *"Anna Christie."* The Anna of *Chris Christophersen* was raised in England, has become a stenographer, and is a "proper" lady. The more familiar Anna of *"Anna Christie,"* by contrast, was raised in Minnesota and became a prostitute.

In *Chris Christophersen*, Paul Andersen, the second mate of the fictitious steamer *"Londonderry,"* was modeled after O'Neill himself, sharing similar physical attributes and history (Comens, vii). It appears that Anna and Paul have qualities of the real Eugene O'Neill, and the character Chris Christophersen, based on the real Christopherson, provides a contrasting context for the expression of those qualities.

In Act Two, Scene One, Anna and Chris are adrift on the coal barge in a fog off Cape Cod. The towline has parted, and they have no way of controlling the movement of their unrigged barge. Chris tells Anna that normally his barge is the first or second in the tow. He talks of receiving his towline from the man on the third barge, a man that he does not trust. As the fourth barge in the tow, they were as much as a mile behind the tug, and in the fog there is no way the tug would know that they had broken loose. O'Neill shows his knowledge of the practices of coastal barges. Chris tells Anna that they are drifting out to sea. "Maybe tide turn and ve drift back ashore on Cape some place" (O'Neill, CP1, 835). O'Neill was well aware that barges commonly washed up on Cape Cod beaches; a number had landed at Peaked Hill Bars.

O'Neill's friend, the real Chris Christopherson, probably worked on a schooner barge rather than an unrigged barge like that of the character Chris. Setting the action of the play on an unrigged barge heightened the drama. Had they been on a schooner barge they would have had the ability to use the rudimentary sails to gain some control of their situation and not be helplessly cast adrift. In addition, there would have been other crew on board a schooner barge, a complication that would have destroyed the intimate interaction and dynamic that develops between Anna and her father in the play.

Chris thinks the trip is a "Jonah voyage." Sailors commonly used the Biblical reference to Jonah when referring to bad luck. Anna responds:

> Don't be superstitious, Father. The trip has been wonderful. Everything's been so jolly—and different—since we left New York. And now—drifting all alone in the fog—I wouldn't miss it for the world. I never knew living on ships was so— different from land. And the sea—I hadn't the slightest idea of what it could mean, before. Why, I'd love to work on it, I know I would, if I were a man. I don't wonder you've always been a sailor" (O'Neill, CP1, 834).

Chris explains to Anna the danger of being adrift in the fog and calls fog one of the sea's "dirty tricks." The tidal current is taking them away from land out into the open sea and into the shipping lanes. A steamer could run the barge down without even knowing it. Chris is unsuccessful in fixing his foghorn, which is the only way in the fog he can make the presence of the barge known. Anna responds:

> But why don't I feel afraid? I ought to, oughtn't I, a girl who's always lived inland? And you've told me what danger we're in. But I don't feel afraid the least bit. I don't feel anything— but—(she gropes helplessly for words) restful—as if I'd found something I'd always been seeking—as if this were the place for me to be—and I feel happy! (exultantly) Yes—happier

than I've ever been anywhere before! *(As Chris makes no comment but a heavy sigh, she continues wonderingly.)* It's queer for me to feel that way, don't you think? (O'Neill, CP1, 840)

O'Neill found great comfort in the sea, whether swimming or in a boat, and Anna appears to be discovering the same type of comfort with the sea, as if there is no way that the sea and fog could bring a single danger. She senses no threat, but sees the sea as nurturing and protecting. Anna shares some of the same feelings expressed by Edmund, the autobiographical character in *Long Day's Journey into Night*. Edmund says: "It was a great mistake, my being born a man, I would have been much more successful as a sea gull or a fish" (O'Neill, CP3, 812).

Act Two, Scene One, ends just prior to the barge being run down by a steamer. O'Neill scripts the moments leading to the collision with great detail and insight into such situations. Chris has Anna put on a life jacket and stand by their small boat. Standing on the deckhouse, Chris shouts:

Ahoy! Ahoy dere! Ahoy on board steamer! *(As through a sudden break in the fog a loud noise of throbbing engines and swishing waves sweeps over the barge. Chris' face is turned toward the bow. He gives a loud yell of angry dismay)* Dere she come! She hit us on port bow sure! Cast off, Anna! *(Lantern in hand he jumps to the deck and leaps madly astern to where the white-faced Anna stands with the painter she has freed from the bit in her hands. He snatches it from her.)* Good gel! *(He grabs her in one arm around the waist, letting the lantern go, and slings her over the port side like a bag of meal.)* Over with you! *(A thin wail sounds from the fog over head: "Barge dead ahead!" Chris stands with one foot on the port bulwark ready to jump, his eyes turned toward the bow. A prolonged, ear-racking blast of the steamer's whistle seems to shatter the fog to fragments as The Curtain Falls)* (O'Neill, CP1, 844).

By the opening of the next scene Anna and Chris have been rescued and brought aboard the steamer *"Londonderry,"* a British tramp steamer bound from Boston to Buenos Aires. Anna meets Paul Andersen, the second mate, who also has found contentment at sea. In Act Two, Scene Two, Andersen tells Anna about his brothers who stayed home to work on the family farm, a job and life that he found stifling. He tells her he went to college for two years and then bummed around the country for a while doing manual labor, then took a job with an insurance company. "I resigned on a sudden hunch and shipped away as a seaman on a tramp steamer—Australia, South Africa, the Far East—all over. Then—and only then—I began to feel the sense of finding home, you speak of. And here I am still—quite contented and unrepentant" (O'Neill, CP1, 857). Andersen's experiences are reminiscent of O'Neill's: a wanderer until he goes to sea. Andersen finds his place working on the sea. O'Neill also found comfort at sea, and then carried it with him, into his writing, where he continued discovering himself.

Anna suggests to Andersen that he work his way up to become a captain of his own ship. Andersen responds:

> Responsibilities! A captain belongs to his ship first, last, and always. So does a first mate. But a second mate belongs to himself.
>
> ANNA: But if they love their ship?
>
> ANDERSEN: Then they don't love themselves enough. The sea doesn't love ships. She plays with them, destroys them, endures them because she expresses herself through them —but they belong to her, not she them (O'Neill, CP1, 860).

Andersen's thoughts about being a second mate as opposed to a captain or first mate exemplify O'Neill's desire for independence and his development of characters that are either second mates, engineers, or junior officers who can maintain a level of independence through limited responsibility. O'Neill also illustrates his understanding of the sea when Andersen speaks of the sea playing with ships. O'Neill had witnessed how insignificant a large ship can be when it is tossed by the sea in a hurricane, or left on the beach after a storm.

Anna and Andersen debate the success of a relationship between a sailor and a woman. Anna talks of her own parents who never saw each other because her father was always at sea. Andersen suggests that times have changed and the days of sail are part of the past. In Act Three, Scene Two, Andersen says:

> Listen Anna, I've found a way to beat your father's bogie stories. You won't have to settle down in a landman's way—to a house and lot. I wouldn't want you to. I wouldn't love you if

you did. I love the you who is different from the rest of the pack—the girl with the sea in her eyes, and the love of it in her blood—the girl who loves and feels the things I love and feel! *(then buoyantly as if the vision of it were clear before her eyes)* We'll not leave the sea, you and I. We'll keep it in spite of everything. And we'll go to all the ports of the world and see them all—together! And the sea shall be our mother, and the mother of our children. And you won't have to wait for me as your mother waited for him—watching and hoping and despairing. No you will be with me, beside me, a part of me—always! (O'Neill, CP1, 885).

O'Neill is suggesting a new age for husband and wife, a new generation. He suggests a time when husband and wife can wander the world together and not be tied down to land and home. But at the end of the play Anna's father accepts the call of the sea and signs on again. Chris is resigned to the fact that the sea has beaten him and there is no use in fighting it. The sea has become his wife and family.

George C. Tyler, the producer of the Abbey Players in New York and James O'Neill's business associate, produced *Chris Christophersen* in 1920. The play was scheduled to try out in Atlantic City and Philadelphia before its move to Broadway. O'Neill had confidence in the director, Frederick Stanhope, because he had "four years' experience before the mast" as a sailor aboard ship (Sheaffer, SA, 7). The play opened in Atlantic City in March, a month after *Beyond the Horizon* opened on Broadway.

Unfortunately, the production never reached Broadway, closing after the Philadelphia engagement. O'Neill blamed Tyler for the failure of the production. Tyler had demanded drastic cuts and cast it poorly. O'Neill also felt that Tyler had tried to make it a popular success rather than treating it sympathetically and allowing it to find its audience (Comens, ix-x). Frustrated, O'Neill advised Tyler to "Throw the present play in the ash barrel. Candidly that is what strikes me as promising the most chance of future success, both artistic and financial" (Comens, ix). Within the year O'Neill went on to rewrite *Chris Christophersen,* and the play was reborn as *"Anna Christie."*

When O'Neill discarded *Chris Christophersen* after the disappointing engagement in Philadelphia and decided to rewrite it, he said to

George C. Tyler, the producer: "In the back of my mind there are already inklings as to how this could be done. . . . Suffice it to say that of the present play I would keep without change only the character of Chris—I'd give you a real daughter and lover, flesh-and-blood people—and the big underlying idea of the sea" (Sheaffer, SA, 10).

In the change from *Chris Christophersen* to *"Anna Christie,"* the play was shortened by two scenes and the number of characters was reduced. Anna becomes the central figure, whereas in the earlier version Chris, Anna, and Andersen shared the focus. The tone of the revised play is darkened by making Anna a prostitute, abused by her relatives in Minnesota, and by making her love interest a stoker, who feels superior to sailors. The action of the play takes place at Johnny the Priest's and aboard the barge *"Simeon Winthrop"* at anchor in Provincetown and Boston harbors. By contrast to *Chris Christophersen*, in *"Anna Christie"* four men from a steamer that has sunk come on board the barge. Another difference between the two plays is that the barge in *"Anna Christie"* is a schooner barge and larger than the unrigged barge in *Chris Christophersen*. The larger barge is in keeping with the real Chris. O'Neill never explicitly states the type of barge, but in the opening act of *"Anna Christie"* Marthy tells Anna that her father is a barge captain with five men working under him, which indicates the type of barge.

Upon completion of the new play, initially titled *The Ole Davil,* O'Neill sent it to Tyler. Tyler felt the play was overwritten, but he decided to option it. He let the option expire before doing anything with the script. O'Neill next gave the script to Broadway producer Arthur Hopkins, who agreed to produce it. O'Neill made a few revisions and renamed it *"Anna Christie."* It opened on Broadway at the Vanderbilt Theatre on 2 November 1921, to great acclaim (Comens, x). O'Neill received his second Pulitzer Prize for this play.

The character of Anna in both *Chris Christophersen* and *"Anna Christie"* shares some of O'Neill's traits. Stephen Black points out that the Anna of *Chris Christophersen* lost her mother at an early age and had been educated away from home according to the conventions of the time. O'Neill similarly had been separated from his mother and educated in boarding schools from an early age. The Anna of *"Anna Christie"* represents the part of O'Neill that rebelled after he learned of his mother's morphine addiction and felt that he had been removed from her a second time (Black, 261).

Anna is the play's central figure and most sympathetic character. Through Anna, O'Neill expresses his feelings about the sea and his fatalistic view of life. When Chris blames himself for his daughter's mistreatment by her relatives and forced entry into prostitution, she says: "There ain't nothing to forgive, anyway. It ain't your fault, and it ain't mine, and it ain't his [Mat's] neither. We're all poor nuts, and things happen, and we yust get mixed in wrong, that's all" (O'Neill, CP1, 1015). O'Neill expresses a similar view in *Long Day's Journey into Night* when, talking to her sons, Mary Tyrone says: "None of us can help the things life has done to us. They're done before you realize it, and once they're done they make you do other things until at last everything comes between you and what you'd like to be, and you've lost your true self forever" (O'Neill, CP3, 749).

Instead of using himself as the inspiration for Anna's love interest, as he did in *Chris Christophersen*, O'Neill modeled Mat Burke after his friend Driscoll, the stoker from the American Line. When Burke first appears in Act Two, O'Neill describes him:

> He is stripped to the waist, has on nothing but a pair of dirty dungaree pants. He is a powerful, broad-chested six-footer, his face handsome in a hard rough, bold, defiant way. He is about thirty, in the full power of his heavy-muscled, immense strength. His dark eyes are bloodshot and wild from sleeplessness. The muscles of his arms and shoulders are lumped in knots and bunches, the veins of his forearms stand out like blue cords (O'Neill, CP1, 984).

In Burke, O'Neill paints an idealized view of his dead friend Driscoll. O'Neill had always been in awe of the confidence, strength, and power that Driscoll exuded. Burke is a tribute to the man that O'Neill had so greatly admired.

O'Neill's other friends, Jimmy the Priest and Chris Christopherson, are portrayed accurately in both *Chris Christophersen* and *"Anna Christie."* The description of Johnny the Priest is almost identical in both plays, an accurate portrait of the real person.

> "Johnny the Priest" deserves his nickname. With his pale, thin, clean-shaven face, mild blue eyes and white hair, a cassock

would seem more suited to him than the apron he wears. Neither his voice nor his general manner dispel this illusion which has made him a personage of the water front. They are soft and bland. But beneath all his mildness one senses the man behind the mask—cynical, callous, hard as nails (O'Neill, CP1, 959).

This was the man O'Neill knew during his days at Jimmy's—the man who would not tolerate trouble, who protected his regulars and ignored their actions when they robbed a transient outside his door. O'Neill took a few liberties with his depiction of Chris, but for the most part he was faithful to the real person. The real Chris was a veteran seaman who had been reduced to a mate on a barge and who referred to the sea as "dat ole davil." The Chris of the plays had the same history and feeling about the sea. The only departure from reality was that O'Neill made him Swedish and a widower who had abandoned his daughter. In reality Christopherson's wife was alive and living in Norway. He returned home every few years to visit his family (Sheaffer, SP, 202).

In Act One of *"Anna Christie,"* Chris takes on a fatherly attitude toward his daughter. He tries to convince her that a trip with him on the barge would be good for her. He says:

> You don't know how nice it's on barge, Anna. Tug come and ve gat towed out on voyage—yust water all round, and sun, and fresh air, and good grub for make you strong, healthy gel. You see many tangs you don't see before. You gat moon-light at night, maybe; see steamer pass; see schooner make sail—see everything dat's pooty. You need take rest like dat. You work too hard for young gel already. You need vacation, yes! (O'Neill, CP1, 976–77)

Chris's words recall O'Neill's own desire and his pleasure at being at sea.

Act Two of the play is set on the barge at anchor in Provincetown Harbor. Mat Burke enters and introduces the friction between sail and steam and between sailor and stoker. Burke makes his feelings clear from the start. He has come aboard the barge after being out in one of his ship's boats, rowing for two days and nights with three shipmates lying in the bottom of the boat unable to lend a hand. As one of the shipmates is carried past Burke he looks at the man with contempt and says: "Is it losing the small wits ye iver had, ye are? Deck-scrubbing scut!" (O'Neill, CP1, 984) "Deck-scrubbing scut" refers to the fact that the shipmate is not a stoker, but a deckhand, who by this period was reduced to performing menial duties and therefore was not as valuable to the ship as a stoker. The incident illustrates the animosity between stokers and sailors that O'Neill witnessed on the American Line. Burke continues to express his superiority over his three shipmates when Anna asks him if he needs to lie down and get some rest. Posturing to impress Anna, he makes it clear to her that he is not weak like the sailors. Later in the play Anna speaks with her father, who refers to Burke as a sailor. Anna is quick to correct him: "He ain't a sailor. He's a stoker." Chris responds: "Dat vas million times vorse, Ay tal you! Dem fallars dat work below shoveling coal vas de dirtiest, rough gang of no-good fallars in vorld!" (O'Neill, CP1, 994). Chris is right in his assessment of the requirements for industrialized labor. The exchange between Chris and his daughter further demonstrates the contempt between the two groups. It also illustrates that Anna is being won over by Burke.

The battle between steam and sail, stoker and sailor, is carried on by Burke and Chris.

> CHRIS: You vas young fool! In ole years when Ay vas on wind-yammer, Ay vas through hundred storms vorse'n dat! Ships vas ships den—and men dat sail on dem was real men. And now what you gat on steamers? You gat fallars don't know ship from mudscow. And below deck you gat fallars yust know how for shovel coal—might yust as vell vork on coal vagon ashore!

> BURKE: Is it casting insults at the men in the stokehole ye are, ye old ape? God stiffen you! Wan of them is worth any ten stock-fish-swilling square-heads ever shipped on a windbag (O'Neill, CP1, 1000).

O'Neill pits the Irish stokers and the Scandinavian sailors of his past against each other. O'Neill is echoing the conflict that had been going on since ocean steamships proved themselves in the 1840s.

THE HAIRY APE

O'Neill continues the battle between sailor and stoker in *The Hairy Ape*. This time, however, it is the Irish sailor, Paddy, who is at odds with the American stoker, Yank. O'Neill wrote *The Hairy Ape* in December 1921, not long after *"Anna Christie"* opened on Broadway. The Provincetown Players' production of *The Hairy Ape* opened on 9 March 1922, the same night O'Neill's mother's body arrived in New York by train from California. *The Hairy Ape* moved to Broadway that April. According to Louis Sheaffer, the opening of *The Hairy Ape* established that O'Neill, at the age of 33, was no longer America's "most promising playwright"; he was now the best playwright the country had ever produced (Sheaffer, SA, 89).

The first four scenes of *The Hairy Ape* take place on board a passenger-carrying steamer. In this play O'Neill draws upon his experience on the American Line, where he first discovered the great animosity between stokers and sailors. O'Neill saw how demeaning life was for sailors compared to the luxurious life of the upper-class passengers. In addition to the posturing of the stoker as an expression of his superiority over sailors, Yank is searching to find the place where he belongs. Through Yank's struggle, O'Neill tries to come to terms with why his friend Driscoll—someone he perceived as strong, confident, and vital—killed himself. O'Neill said that his search for an answer to Driscoll's death provided the idea for *The Hairy Ape*. Yank embodies O'Neill's essential view of Driscoll, a man destined for an untimely end, while Mat Burke of *"Anna Christie"* is a romanticized view of his friend (Sheaffer, SA, 73).

In the first four scenes of *The Hairy Ape,* Yank dominates his shipmates in the fo'c's'le and the stokehold. Through his charisma, strength, and enthusiasm he becomes their unofficial leader. Yank feels at home in the environment. He is part of the ship, a vital element that helps the machine operate. The other stokers in the fo'c's'le do not command the attention that Yank does. Long and Paddy suggest that they might be able to dominate the fo'c's'le, but Yank makes it clear that they do not fit in as well as he does. Long is an intellectual and a revolutionary, which isolates him from the others in the fo'c's'le and the workings of the ship. Paddy constantly looks back to the days of sail and mourns its passing. Yank responds: "I belong and he don't. He's dead but I'm livin'" (O'Neill, CP2,

128). Reminiscent of Chris Christopherson, Paddy is from that past age of sail, an age that has gone by.

In Scene One, Yank says that the men of the stokehold are the important men, the ones that make the ship go, and that no one else is important (O'Neill, CP2, 125). Paddy responds with a nostalgic speech, which alludes to O'Neill's experiences aboard the *Charles Racine:* "Oh, to be back in the fine days of my youth, onchone! Oh, there was fine beautiful ships them days—clippers wid tall masts touching the sky—fine strong men in them—men that was sons of the sea as if 'twas the mother that bore them" (O'Neill, CP2, 126).

Paddy continues on about the setting of sails and singing of chanteys to help with the work, and the freedom the men felt as they sailed away from land and the sunset behind them. "Oh, to be scudding

1922 production of *The Hairy Ape* with Carlotta Monterey (center) as Mildred and Louis Wolheim as Yank (Sheaffer-O'Neill Collection, Connecticut College)

south again wid the power of the Trade Wind driving her on steady through the nights and the days! Full sail on her! Nights and days!" He talks of the sky filled with stars or the full moon and the "sails stretching aloft all silver and white, not a sound on the deck." He speaks of the work being hard, but work with "skill and daring to it." He reminisces of the dog-watches, when a sailor can sit back and smoke his pipe, and when the look-out spots land, "and we see the mountains of South Americy wid the red fire of the setting sun painting their white tops and the clouds floating by them!" (O'Neill, CP2, 126–27). Paddy's speech is a romanticized view of working aboard a sailing ship, but it is based on the reality O'Neill had experienced and seen for himself.

Paddy pulls himself out of his nostalgia and ends his speech by saying to Yank:

> what's the use of talking? 'Tis a dead man's whisper. *(to Yank resentfully)* 'Twas them days men belonged to ships not now. 'Twas them days a ship was part of the sea, and a man was part of a ship, and the sea joined all together and made it one. *(scornfully)* Is it one wid this you'd be, Yank—black smoke from the funnels smudging the sea, smudging the decks—the bloody engines pounding and throbbing and shaking—wid divil a sight of sun or a breath of clean air— choking our lungs wid coal dust—breaking our backs and hearts in the hell of the stokehole—feeding the bloody fur- nace—feeding our lives along wid the coal, I'm thinking— caged in by steel from sight of the sky like bloody apes in the Zoo! *(with a harsh laugh)* Ho-ho, divil mend you! Is it to belong to that you're wishing? Is it a flesh and blood wheel of the engines you'd be? (O'Neill, CP2, 127)

Yank's response to Paddy is a simple one: "Sure ting! Dat's me. What about it?" (O'Neill, CP2, 127). Yank accuses Paddy of being a dead rem- nant of the past who no longer belongs, while he, Yank, belongs to the present and is the living. During Scene Three, in the stokehold, Paddy is almost defeated by the work while Yank is invigorated by it.

The irony is that, from that moment on, Yank progresses toward the discovery that he does not belong and never has. Scene Four, the final scene that takes place on board ship, ends with Yank in a rage and the men of the fo'c's'le restraining him. Paddy is in a position of control over Yank when he tells the men to keep him down, illustrating that the sailor of the past has a place in society because he is more than just part of the mechanism that makes the ship move. Yank, in his final speech of the play, taking Paddy's analogy to heart, speaks to an ape in the zoo, describing his day, which he has spent free of his usual place in the dark of the stokehold and fo'c's'le or waterfront bar. He has been at the Battery in New York City, watching the sun come up, seeing the pretty colors, and watching the ships coming and going in the harbor. He has felt the warmth of the sun. Yank tells the ape that he now realizes that Paddy is right, Yank cannot fit in (O'Neill, CP2, 161). O'Neill is expressing his respect and admiration for the sailors of the great sailing ships, while grappling with what could have driven Driscoll, a man of apparently boundless strength, to take his own life. O'Neill's answer to the suicide question lies in Yank's inability to find a place where he belongs as a human being because society has reduced him to the equivalent of an animal in a zoo. For a while Yank draws his strength from the belief that he belongs in the stokehold, where he is part of the steam engine. But being human, made of flesh and blood, he can never really be part of the engine. Yank finally finds acceptance, peace, and a sense of belonging in death—crushed in the arms of the ape.

It took O'Neill about two and a half weeks to write *The Hairy Ape,* but the story had been developing in his mind for years (Sheaffer, SA, 73). According to Sheaffer, O'Neill wrote the play entirely out of himself, out of his heart. It was based on Driscoll, but it is also about himself, a man forever haunted by feelings of not belonging (Sheaffer, SP, 389). Arthur Hopkins, reviewing O'Neill's career in 1947, wrote: "In my opinion *The Hairy Ape* remains O'Neill's most important work. This is true O'Neill, the inspired dramatic poet. Here are perception, compassion and prophecy. The world today is full of desperate Yanks, frantically determined to destroy an inhuman scheme that provides no place for them" (Sheaffer, SA, 89).

MOURNING BECOMES ELECTRA
AND "THE CALMS OF CAPRICORN"

After *The Hairy Ape,* O'Neill turned away from writing about the maritime world and explored other themes. But in the late 1920s and into the 1930s he again returned to the sea for inspiration. He wrote *Mourning Becomes Electra* and developed the lengthy scenario for "The Calms of Capricorn." Both of the plays are set in the era when clipper ships ruled the seas, the peak of the great age of sail. It is a period that many, including O'Neill, looked back on with great nostalgia, the time of "wooden ships and iron men." *Mourning Becomes Electra* is set in 1865–66, the end of the clipper ship period. One of its acts takes place on board the fictitious clipper *"Flying Trades."* "The Calms of Capricorn," set in 1857, the middle of the clipper era, takes place almost entirely aboard the clipper *"Dream of the West."* Carlotta Monterey, O'Neill's third wife, made a few entries in her diary regarding O'Neill's interest in clipper ships: 12 May 1930, "Gene reading book on Clipper Ships"; 6 August 1930, "buys marvelous books on Clipper Ships"; 16 March 1931, "discusses writing Clipper Ship play next!" (O'Neill, Calms, vii). O'Neill began working on *Mourning Becomes Electra* in 1929 and finished the trilogy in early 1931. By June of that year he had begun to write down some of his ideas for "The Calms of Capricorn" (O'Neill, Calms, vii). *Mourning Becomes Electra* opened in New York in October 1931 to great critical acclaim.

Looking back to Greek tragedy, O'Neill based *Mourning Becomes Electra* on the *Oresteia* trilogy of Aeschylus and created a New England tragedy set in the aftermath of the Civil War. It is a story of adultery, murder, and incest. O'Neill titled the three parts of the trilogy *Homecoming, The Hunted,* and *The Haunted.* The action takes place at the Mannon family residence in a small New England seaport town, with the exception of Act Four of the second play, which is set aboard the *"Flying Trades."* The action that takes place on the ship is at the center of the trilogy, highlighting the fact that the sea is integral to the life of the Mannon family, but also that the sea symbolizes escape and freedom to members of the family. O'Neill probably derived the name of the ship, *"Flying Trades,"* from the real clipper ship *Flying Cloud.* One of the most famous of the nearly 450 American clippers, the *Flying Cloud* held the record, well into the twentieth century, for the fastest passages around Cape Horn from New York to San Francisco and from New York to Hong Kong, via San Francisco (Howe, 192).

The characters of the play, the Mannon home, and other references in the play were derived from New London people, places, and history. In particular, the Mannon family home is a reminder of four Greek Revival houses built in a row on Huntington Street in New London by Ezra Chappel between 1835 and 1845. New London residents dubbed the houses Whale Oil Row, reflecting that the wealth of the original owners came from the whaling industry. O'Neill describes the set at the opening of Act One of the first play, *Homecoming:*

> Exterior of the Mannon house on a late afternoon in April, 1865. . . . Behind the driveway the white Grecian temple portico with its six tall columns extends across the stage. . . . The white columns cast black bars of shadow on the gray wall behind them. The windows of the lower floor reflect the sun's rays in a resentful glare. The temple portico is like an incongruous white mask fixed on the house to hide its somber gray ugliness (O'Neill, CP2, 893).

Other New London landmarks are referenced in the play. Later in Act Three of *Homecoming,* the stage directions state: *"The boom of a cannon sounds from the fort that guards the harbor"* (O'Neill, CP2, 926). O'Neill is referring to Fort Trumbull, which was not far from his family home.

O'Neill makes a historical reference to New London early in Act One, when Seth responds to a query from Minnie, a townsperson, about the Mannons' wealth: "Ezra's made a pile, and before him, his father, Abe Mannon, he inherited some and made a pile more in shippin'. Started one of the fust Western Ocean packet lines" (O'Neill, CP2, 895).

The primary characters in the play are Ezra Mannon, his wife Christine, their children Lavinia and Orin, Captain Adam Brant of the *"Flying Trades,"* and the Mannon's gardener Seth Beckwith. A number of minor characters represent townspeople and act as a chorus similar to those in Greek tragedies. O'Neill refers to them in the stage directions as "types of townsfolk rather than individuals, a chorus representing the town come to look and listen and spy on the rich exclusive Mannons" (O'Neill, CP2, 894). Seth, the gardener, is a bridge between the townspeople and the Mannons. He interacts with both and is able to provide some information and commentary for the other characters and audience.

O'Neill uses three characters to reinforce the plays' connection to the sea and to express his love of the sea and ships. They are Seth, Captain Brant, and the Chantyman, who appears briefly in the *The Hunted*. Captain Brant is a pivotal character. He is the son of Ezra's brother and one of the Mannon household servants. Brant's parents were forced to leave the household when their relationship was discovered. Initially, Brant returns to exact revenge on the family by having an affair with Christine, but they actually fall in love. When Brant arrives at the Mannon home he says that he is there to court Lavinia, but in reality it is to be close to Christine. Brant speaks to Lavinia about his love for his ship:

> I'm afraid I gabbed too much that night. Maybe I bored you with my talk of clipper ships and my love for them?
>
> LAVINIA: *(dryly)* "Tall, white clippers," you called them. You said they were like beautiful, pale women to you. You said you loved them more than you'd ever loved a woman (O'Neill, CP2, 909).

Brant's passion for clipper ships is reminiscent of Paddy's love for sailing ships in *The Hairy Ape*.

Throughout the play, O'Neill has the opportunity to display his knowledge and love of sea chanteys, and he relies on them to reinforce the maritime context of the play. The chanteys are sung by Seth, the Chantyman, and Joe Silva. Silva is one of the townspeople in the final part of the trilogy. O'Neill probably drew on the Portuguese fishermen of Provincetown for the development of the character of Silva.

Seth sings one of the most popular capstan chanteys, "Shenandoah." This slow, melodic chantey is a powerful tool for O'Neill. The haunting chantey is one of the first things the audience hears at the opening of *Homecoming* and one of the last to be heard at the end of *The Haunted*. The stage directions at the beginning of the play explain:

> *a man's voice is heard singing the chanty "Shenandoah"—a song that more than any other holds in it the brooding rhythm of the sea. The voice grows quickly nearer. It is thin and aged, the wraith of what must once have been a good baritone.*

"Oh, Shenandoah, I long to hear you
A-way, my rolling river
Oh, Shenandoah, I can't get near you
Way-ay, I'm bound away
Across the wide Missouri."

The singer, Seth Beckwith, finishes the last line as he enters from around the corner of the house (O'Neill, CP2, 893–94).

There are a number of versions of the song, but O'Neill uses the most common opening verse. The song has a mysterious and mournful quality, an expression of longing and unfulfilled desire, while at the same time expressing an understanding of love and passion. The song captures the essence of what troubles the members of the Mannon family and at the same time provides a continual reminder of the family and the town's connection to the sea, and of Christine and Lavinia's desire to escape from the confines of the household.

O'Neill uses "Shenandoah" again in Act Four of *The Hunted,* which is the only act of the trilogy that does not take place at the Mannon home, but on the wharf and part of the deck of the *"Flying Trades,"* docked in Boston. At the opening of the act the stage directions state:

Borne on the wind the melancholy refrain of the capstan chanty "Shenandoah," sung by a chantyman with the crew coming in on the chorus, drifts over the water from a ship that is weighing anchor in the harbor (O'Neill, CP2, 984).

The Chantyman is lying in the shadows on the wharf and comments on what he is hearing: "A hell of a chantyman that feller be! Screech owls is op'ry singers compared to him! I'll give him a taste of how "Shenandoah" ought t' be sung!" (O'Neill, CP2, 984). He sings the same version that Seth has sung earlier in the play and continues with a second verse: "Oh, Shenandoah, I love your daughter; A-way, my rolling river!" (O'Neill, CP2, 985). After commenting on his own lack of ability with the song, because he has had too much to drink, he sings another chantey:

"A bottle o' wine and a bottle o' beer
And a bottle of Irish whiskey oh!
So early in the morning
The sailor likes his bottle oh!" (O'Neill, CP2, 985).

When the Chantyman's singing brings Brant out on deck, wondering what the noise is, they get into conversation and the Chantyman extols his talents. Brant responds:

> I'm not doubting your ability. But I'd advise you turn in and sleep it off.

> CHANTYMAN: *(not heeding this—sadly)* Aye, but it ain't fur long, steam is comin' in, the sea is full o' smoky teakettles, the old days is dyin', an' where'll you an' me be then? *(lugubriously drunken again)* Everything is dyin'! Abe Lincoln is dead. I used to ship on the Mannon packets an' I seed in the paper where Ezra Mannon was dead! *(Brant starts guiltily. The chantyman goes on maudlinly.)* Heart failure killed him, it said, but I know better! I've sailed on Mannon hookers an' been worked t' death and gotten swill fur grub, an' I know he didn't have no heart in him! Open him up an' you'd find a dried turnip! The old skinflint must have left a pile o' money. Who gits it, I wonder? Leave a widder, did he? (O'Neill, CP2, 987).

O'Neill uses the Chantyman to express a number of things here. One is O'Neill's familiar lament regarding sail versus steam. But the Chantyman is also inadvertently confronting Brant about having an affair with Christine and acquiring the poison that Christine used to murder her husband, Ezra, in Act Four of the *Homecoming*. The double meaning of the word "hooker"—both a term of derisive endearment for a ship and a slang term for a prostitute—alludes to Christine's affair with Brant.

Before he leaves, the Chantyman sings one more chantey for Brant in an effort to convince him that he should hire a chantyman for the *"Flying Trades."* O'Neill has the Chantyman sing a halyard chantey that offers further commentary on the Mannons and Brant.

> "Oh, they call me Hanging Johnny
> Away–ay–i–oh!
> They says I hangs for money
> Oh, hang, boys, hang!"

Brant tells the Chantyman to leave, and as he exits the Chantyman continues to sing:

> "They say I hanged my mother
> Away–ay–i–oh!

They say I hanged my mother
Oh, hang, boys, hang!" (O'Neill, CP2, 988).

O'Neill's use of the chantey "Hanging Johnny" can be seen as a way of tormenting Brant, but, in the style of Greek tragedy, it also is foretelling events that will occur in the last act of *The Hunted*.

In the final act of *The Hunted* Seth sings the first verse of "Shenandoah" again, but he is cut off by the sound of a pistol shot from inside the house. Christine has been driven to commit suicide. Orin is distraught over his mother's death, and his sister Lavinia soothes him:

Ssshh! Ssshh! You have me, haven't you? I love you. I'll help you to forget. *(. . . Seth's voice comes from the drive, right, close at hand:*
    "She's far across the stormy water
    Way-ay, I'm bound away—"
He enters right, front. Lavinia turns to him.)

SETH: *(approaching)* Say, Vinnie, did you hear a shot–?

LAVINIA: *(sharply)* I want you to go get Doctor Blake. Tell him Mother has killed herself in a fit of insane grief over Father's death (O'Neill, CP2, 1003).

Seth's second verse of "Shenandoah" suggests that in death Christine has been able to escape the haunted Mannon household. At the end of the trilogy O'Neill uses the song in a similar way. While looking at Lavinia, Seth sings: "Oh, Shenandoah, I can't get near you; Way-ay, I'm bound away." Lavinia looks at him and responds: "I'm not bound away—not now, Seth. I'm bound here—to the Mannon dead!" (O'Neill, CP2, 1053). Lavinia is trapped and has no place to go. This final moment of the trilogy is the only time when a character responds directly to the meaning of the chantey's lyrics.

While O'Neill was finishing *Mourning Becomes Electra,* he got the idea to write a play set entirely on board a clipper ship. Clipper ships epitomized the great age of sail, of which he had fond memories and a romantic view. It was also a way for O'Neill to tell some of his favorite stories of the men he knew when he went to sea and during the days he lived at Jimmy the Priest's. On 20 June 1931 O'Neill wrote in his notebook: "Play whole action of which takes place on clipper ship bound

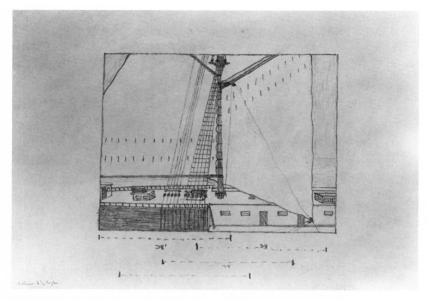

O'Neill's design for the set of "The Calms of Capricorn," Act 4, Scene 1 (Yale Collection of American Literature, Beinecke Rare Book and Manuscript Library)

round the horn and winds up in Shanghai Brown's boarding house in Frisco—what year best (?)—look up data on Shanghai Brown, if any" (O'Neill, Calms, vii).

He made further notes over the next few of years. During that time O'Neill commissioned a number of models of clipper ships, including the *Lightning, Flying Cloud, James Baines,* and possibly *Sovereign of the Seas,* by Donald Pace, a model-maker in New York City. All of the ships were famous in their day and exemplified the finest ship designs. O'Neill wrote to the model-maker asking detailed questions about size and design of the original ships, designed and built by Donald McKay, and went on to say: "You won't mind my going into this matter so at length, I know. You see, one of my greatest interests in selecting these models is to have before me, comparatively, the changes in McKay design in his fastest ships, to have them all on tables side by side."[46]

The models would have been with O'Neill while he worked on "The Calms of Capricorn." O'Neill also made detailed drawings for the set of the play, which accurately depict the clipper ship. O'Neill refers to the *Flying Cloud* in the opening of Act Four of the scenario, when everyone talks excitedly about how their ship might have beaten the *Flying Cloud*'s record from New York to San Francisco.

Originally, "The Calms of Capricorn" was to be the first in a four-play cycle that revolved around a New England family. But by 1935 the idea had evolved into a seven-play cycle, and a few years later it developed further to nine plays. They were to cover different periods in the history of the Harford family. "The Calms of the Capricorn" would have been the fifth of the cycle. The two preceding plays were *A Touch of the Poet,* which O'Neill completed, and *More Stately Mansions.* O'Neill thought he had destroyed the latter play, but it was "finished" by others after his death and presented as "by O'Neill" (Gelbs, LWMC, 722) in New York in 1967. In 1949, O'Neill admitted that he could no longer write. Later, while living in Marblehead, he destroyed the notes and drafts of the cycle plays. However, a good portion of the material survived and was sent to Yale University, including the scenario for "The Calms of Capricorn."

The scenario includes details of the location of each scene, descriptions of characters, and bits of dialogue. The majority of the play is set on board the clipper ship *"Dream of the West,"* with the exception of the first act. The scenario of the play does not end in the boardinghouse of Shanghai Brown as O'Neill had originally planned. It ends on board the ship at anchor in San Francisco Harbor. As with many of his other plays, O'Neill reached into his own experiences for inspiration and authenticity. Scenes One, Two, and Three of Act Three, are all set on board the clipper ship, becalmed in the South Atlantic. This is the same area where the *Charles Racine* was becalmed. The central character is Ethan Harford, who at the beginning of the play is second mate of the *"Dream of the West."* He is described as having "a touch of the poet in him" (O'Neill, Calms, 133). Like the second mate or second engineer characters in O'Neill's other plays, Ethan bears a resemblance to the playwright. In his notes for the second act, O'Neill, refers to Ethan, saying: "He explains bitter dissatisfaction with present life—sea meant freedom from all land values—but he finds himself enslaved by them—always obeying orders —also feels love for the sea & hates it for it" (O'Neill, Calms, 135). O'Neill is expounding on the love/hate relationship that many sailors had with the sea.

In conversation with his mother Ethan says:

O'Neill in Bermuda, ca. 1927 (Sheaffer–O'Neill Collection, Connecticut College)

And I speak to you in symbols which neither of us can think but which our hearts understand, because I love you, and because I love and hate the sea, which you can understand, being also a mother. For the sea is the mother of life—is a woman of all moods for all men, and all seductive & evil—devil mother or wife or mistress or daughter or water-front drab—and it is a sign and symbol of freedom to me that someday as captain of a ship I shall fight her storms and calms and fogs and cross-currents and capricious airs and make a voyage around the Horn to the Golden Gate than ever man has made . . . (O'Neill, Calms, 136)

First Mate Hull falls ill and Ethan is promoted to replace him, but just prior to the ship's departure Hull arrives and Ethan must resume his lesser position. The ship has a few passengers on board, including Ethan's mother Sara, the captain's wife Nancy, and Leda. The women discuss Hull's ingrained dislike of Ethan, suggesting that his last minute arrival was purposeful, to spite Ethan and keep him from advancing.

Leda says, "perhaps he'll [Hull] fall overboard or we can give him a push" (O'Neill, Calms, 147). During a confrontation with Hull, in front of the women, Ethan hits the mate. Hull falls, hits his head, and dies. The women decide to lie and say that Hull fell while coming down the companionway and died. Here, O'Neill might well be inspired by the story that he cut out of the early version of *Bound East for Cardiff*, where Driscoll tells Yank about the harsh mate who disappeared during a voyage.

During the course of the play, Ethan becomes romantically involved with the captain's wife Nancy. Unlike most of O'Neill's second officer characters, Ethan aspires to become captain. Captain Payne becomes ill and takes to his bed. At the end of Act Three, Scene Three, "[Nancy] goes in—sees Ethan advancing with a pillow—says fiercely 'No! Give me what is mine!' snatches it from his hands—leaps at Payne & shoves pillow over his face" (O'Neill, Calms, 174).

At the end of the play Ethan and Nancy exit the scene hand in hand and he says to her: "We'll swim out together—until the fog lifts. And then the sea will alight with beauty forever more—because you are you" (O'Neill, Calms, 186). They commit suicide in the fashion that O'Neill had discussed so often as an ideal way to die.

O'Neill draped in seaweed at Peaked Hill Bars, ca. 1920 (Sheaffer–O'Neill Collection, Connecticut College)

Conclusion

In 1920, at the age of 32, O'Neill said to Olin Downes, who wrote for the *Boston Sunday Post,* "my real start as a dramatist was when I got out of an academy and among men, on the sea" (Estrin, 10). At the time, O'Neill was viewed as one of America's leading playwrights based on the performance and publication of his one-act sea plays. He was the first American playwright to take up realism and devote his work to the portrayal of the average man and the working class.

O'Neill, like his character Yank, never really had a home and was forever looking for a place where he felt he could belong. When Professor Sophus Winther interviewed O'Neill in 1944, O'Neill told him, "I have never had a home, never had a chance to establish roots. I grew up in hotels. My mother never had a home. *Long Day's Journey* is her story and my autobiography. It's strange, but the time I spent at sea on a sailing ship was the *only* time I ever felt I had roots in any place" (Sheaffer, SA, 553). Around the same time, while living in California, O'Neill wrote to a friend and expressed how much he longed to be back by the sea. "Beach grass is the only verdure I really understand, dunes are my hills, the beach-sun is my only sun and the sea is the symbol of the mystery of life to which I belong, and has been that for me since I was a small boy" (Sheaffer, SA, 611).

Eugene O'Neill had always been attracted to the water, so it is not surprising that he sought the sea, or that the two years he spent living and working among sailors in Buenos Aires and New York and aboard the *Charles Racine, SS Ikala, SS New York* and SS *Philadelphia* had a profound impact on his life and work. Two years is a short time in a man's life, but the impact on O'Neill was tremendous. Aboard the *Charles Racine,* one of the last windjammers, under the command of Captain Gustav Waage, one of the last great sailing ship captains, O'Neill found a sense of home—a home filled with sailors for brothers, men he could trust. The lingering echoes of that brief maritime sojourn filled and sustained him and launched his career as America's greatest playwright.

Notes

1. Eugene O'Neill, 325 Pequot Avenue, New London, Connecticut, to Marion Welch, 5 August 1905, Yale Collection of American Literature, Beinecke Rare Book and Manuscript Library, Yale University, published in *Selected Letters of Eugene O'Neill,* Travis Bogard and Jackson R. Bryer, editors, p. 12.
2. Gustav Waage, Boston Roads, to Sigval Bergesen, Stavanger, Norway, 7 June 1910, Sheaffer-O'Neill Collection.
3. Severin Waage, Flekkefjord, Norway, to Louis Sheaffer, 8 March 1962, Sheaffer-O'Neill Collection.
4. Gustav Waage, Boston Roads, to Sigval Bergesen, Stavanger, Norway, 7 June 1910, Sheaffer-O'Neill Collection.
5. Severin Waage, Flekkefjord, Norway, to Louis Sheaffer, 25 June 1958, Sheaffer-O'Neill Collection.
6. Crew list of the *Charles Racine,* Boston to Buenos Aires, 6 June–5 August 1910, Sheaffer-O'Neill Collection.
7. Severin Waage, Flekkefjord, Norway, to Louis Sheaffer, 16 July 1958, Sheaffer-O'Neill Collection.
8. Osmund Christophersen, Stavanger, Norway, to Louis Sheaffer, 22 August 1957, Sheaffer-O'Neill Collection.
9 Severin Waage, Flekkefjord, Norway, to Louis Sheaffer, 25 June 1958, Sheaffer-O'Neill Collection.
10. Ibid.
11. Rolf Skjorestad, Stavanger, Norway, to Louis Sheaffer, [not dated], Sheaffer-O'Neill Collection.
12. Severin Waage, Flekkefjord, Norway, to Louis Sheaffer, 25 June 1958, Sheaffer-O'Neill Collection.
13. Osmund Christophersen, Stavanger, Norway, to Louis Sheaffer, 20 December 1957, Sheaffer-O'Neill Collection.
14. Ibid.
15. Log of *Charles Racine* (transcription), Sheaffer-O'Neill Collection.
16. Ibid.
17. Ibid.
18. Ibid.
19. Osmund Christophersen, Stavanger, Norway, to Louis Sheaffer, 22 August 1957, Sheaffer-O'Neill Collection.
20. Ibid.
21. Osmund Christophersen, Stavanger, Norway, to Louis Sheaffer, 20 December 1957, Sheaffer-O'Neill Collection.
22. Severin Waage, Flekkefjord, Norway, to Louis Sheaffer, (no date), Sheaffer-O'Neill Collection.
23. Severin Waage, Flekkefjord, Norway, to Louis Sheaffer, 4 August 1958, Sheaffer-O'Neill Collection.
24. In the 1890s the United States Shipping Commission discontinued this practice (Quinn, 25).
25. Severin Waage, Flekkefjord, Norway, to Louis Sheaffer, 25 June 1958, Sheaffer-O'Neill Collection.
26. Severin Waage, Flekkefjord, Norway, to Louis Sheaffer, 16 March 1962, Sheaffer-O'Neill Collection.
27. Frederick Hettman, Buenos Aires, Argentina, to Louis Sheaffer, 9 June 1958, Sheaffer-O'Neill Collection.
28. Osmund Christophersen, Stavanger, Norway, to Louis Sheaffer, 22 August 1957, Sheaffer-O'Neill Collection.
29. Agreement and Account of the Crew of the SS *Ikala* (photocopy), Sheaffer-O'Neill Collection.
30. [Cornish],Office of the Registrar General, Ministry of Transportation and Civil Aviation, Cardiff, Great Britain, to Louis Sheaffer,

19 November 1957, Sheaffer-O'Neill Collection.

31. Eugene O'Neill, Tao House, Danville, California, to Dudley Nichols, 27 April 1940, Yale Collection of American Literature, Beinecke Rare Book and Manuscript Library, Yale University, published in *Selected Letters of Eugene O'Neill,* Travis Bogard and Jackson R. Bryer, editors, p. 503.

32. Agreement and Account of the Crew of the SS *Ikala,* (photocopy), Sheaffer-O'Neill Collection.

33. Mutual Release for the Crew of the SS *Philadelphia,* 26 August 1911 (photocopy), Sheaffer-O'Neill Collection.

34. Ibid.

35. Research notes and transcription of police report regarding Chris Christopherson's death, Sheaffer-O'Neill Collection.

36. Black argues, however, that O'Neill's suicide attempt and the effects of the Veronal would have been life threatening, requiring that O'Neill's stomach be pumped and he probably be kept for a few days at Bellevue Hospital (Black, 119–20). Years later O'Neill gave an account of the incident, saying that after his friends had revived him they decided to take him to the hospital. At Bellevue the doctor mistook the situation and told O'Neill not to worry about his friends, they were then taken to the detoxification ward. According to O'Neill the cab driver who took O'Neill back to Jimmy's held the same opinion as the doctor (Sheaffer, SP, 210).

37. [Cornish],Office of the Registrar General, Board of Trade, Cardiff, Great Britain, to Louis Sheaffer, March 1965, Sheaffer-O'Neill Collection.

38. Eugene O'Neill, 325 Pequot Avenue, New London, Connecticut, to David Russell Lyman, Summer 1914, Yale Collection of American Literature, Beinecke Rare Book and Manuscript Library, Yale University, published in *Selected Letters of Eugene O'Neill,* Travis Bogard and Jackson R. Bryer, editors, p. 25.

39. Eugene O'Neill, West Point Pleasant, New Jersey, to John Francis, Provincetown, Massachusetts, 24 December 1918, Sheaffer-O'Neill Collection.

40. Eugene O'Neill, West Point Pleasant, New Jersey, to John Francis, Provincetown, Massachusetts, 8 March 1919, Sheaffer-O'Neill Collection.

41. Eugene O'Neill, "Campsea," South Shore, Bermuda, to John Francis, Provincetown, Massachusetts, 18 February 1925, Sheaffer-O'Neill Collection.

42. Eugene O'Neill, Provincetown, Massachusetts, to H.L. Mencken, 26 May 1917, permission granted by the Enoch Pratt Free Library, Baltimore, Maryland, in accordance with the terms of the bequest of H.L. Mencken. Letter published in *Selected Letters of Eugene O'Neill,* Travis Bogard and Jackson R. Bryer, editors, p. 79.

43. Eugene O'Neill, Sea Island, Georgia, to Richard Dana Skinner, July 1934, Yale Collection of American Literature, Beinecke Rare Book and Manuscript Library, Yale University, published in *Selected Letters of Eugene O'Neill,* Travis Bogard and Jackson R. Bryer, editors, p. 438.

44. Eugene O'Neill, West Point Pleasant, New Jersey, to Barrett H. Clark, 8 May 1919, Yale Collection of American Literature, Beinecke Rare Book and Manuscript Library, Yale University, published in *Selected Letters of Eugene O'Neill,* Travis Bogard and Jackson R. Bryer, editors, p. 87.

45. See Lisa Norling's *Captain Ahab Had a Wife* for information on whaling wives' impact on their communities.

46. Eugene O'Neill, Casa Genotta, Sea Island, Georgia, to Donald Pace, 7 May 1934, Miscellaneous Manuscripts [M194.2], George J. Mitchell Dept. of Special Collections & Archives, Bowdoin College Library, published in *Selected Letters of Eugene O'Neill,* Travis Bogard and Jackson R. Bryer, editors, p. 434.

Chronology

1877 James O'Neill and Mary Ellen Quinlan (Ella) are married.

1878 James O'Neill Jr. (Jamie) born.

1883 Edmund O'Neill born.

1884 James and Ella O'Neill purchase property in New London, Connecticut, which would become their summer home.

1885 Edmund O'Neill dies from measles.

1888 Eugene O'Neill born 16 October at the Barrett House in New York City.

1895 Enters St. Aloysius Academy for Boys, Bronx, New York.

1900 Enters De La Salle Institute, New York City as a day student.

1902 Enters Betts Academy, Stamford, Connecticut.

1906 Enters Princeton University. Does not finish a full academic year.

1909 Marries Kathleen Jenkins. Goes prospecting for gold in Honduras.

1910 Eugene O'Neill Jr. born. O'Neill becomes assistant stage manager of James O'Neill's road company's production of *The White Sister*. In the summer he sails from Boston on the Norwegian bark *Charles Racine* for Buenos Aires. Upon landing he leaves the ship, has various menial jobs, and ultimately lives on the waterfront.

1911 In the spring he returns to New York City aboard the British tramp steamer SS *Ikala*. In New York lives at Jimmy the Priest's sailors' flophouse near the waterfront. In the summer ships as an ordinary seaman on SS *New York* to England and returns on SS *Philadelphia* as an able bodied seaman.

1912 Returns to New London and begins working for the *New London Telegraph*. Eugene and Kathleen are divorced. Enters Gaylord Farm, a tuberculosis sanatorium, on 24 December and stays for six months.

1913 He continues his convalescence in New London. Writes four one-act plays, including *Thirst* and *Warnings*.

1914 Ella O'Neill overcomes her morphine addiction. James O'Neill pays for the publication of *Thirst and Other One Act Plays*, a volume of five one act plays. Eugene O'Neill writes two full-length plays and four one-act plays, including *Fog* and *Children of the Sea (Bound East for Cardiff)*. In the fall he attends George Pierce Baker's workshop in playwriting at Harvard.

1915 Continues in Baker's course for the spring semester. Writes *The Personal Equation*. He returns to New London for part of the summer.

1916 He summers in Provincetown, Massachusetts. At the Wharf Theater in Provincetown the Provincetown Players produce his plays *Bound East for Cardiff, Thirst*, and *Before Breakfast. Bound East for Cardiff* staged in New York in the fall.

1917 While in Provincetown writes *In the Zone, Ile, The Long Voyage Home,* and *The Moon of the Caribbees.* In New York City the Provincetown Players produce *Fog, The Sniper, Before Breakfast, Ile,* and *The Long Voyage Home.* Short story "Tomorrow" is published in *Seven Arts* magazine.

1918 In Greenwich Village O'Neill meets Agnes Boulton. They move to Provincetown and are married on 12 April. Move to West Point Pleasant, New Jersey, for the winter.

1919 Eugene and Agnes move into the converted Coast Guard Station at Peaked Hill Bars, which James O'Neill purchased for the couple. Completes *Beyond the Horizon. The Moon of the Caribbees and Six Other Plays of the Sea* is published. Completes *Chris Christophersen.* Son, Shane Rudraighe, is born.

1920 *Beyond the Horizon* is produced on Broadway and is awarded the Pulitzer Prize. *Chris Christophersen* closes out of town. James O'Neill dies and is buried in Saint Mary's Cemetery in New London. *The Emperor Jones* is produced.

1921 *Gold, The Straw,* and *"Anna Christie"* are produced in New York.

1922 Ella O'Neill dies in California and is buried in Saint Mary's Cemetery, New London. *The First Man* and *The Hairy Ape* are produced. *"Anna Christie"* wins the Pulitzer Prize. O'Neill is visited by Eugene Jr.

1923 James (Jamie) O'Neill Jr. dies and is buried in St. Mary's Cemetery, New London.

1924 *Welded, All Gods Children Got Wings, The Ancient Mariner,* and *Desire Under the Elms* are produced.

1925 Eugene and Agnes O'Neill move to Bermuda. Daughter Oona is born. *The Fountain* is produced.

1926 *The Great God Brown* is produced. Eugene and Agnes purchase a home in Bermuda. Begins his relationship with Carlotta Monterey.

1927 Eugene Jr. enters Yale University.

1928 *Lazarus Laughed, Marco Millions,* and *Strange Interlude* are produced. O'Neill is awarded his third Pulitzer Prize for *Strange Interlude.* Travels abroad with Carlotta. Eugene and Agnes are divorced.

1929 *Dynamo* is produced. O'Neill marries Carlotta in Paris. They lease Chateau du Plessis for their home.

1931 The O'Neills return to the United States. *Mourning Becomes Electra* is produced.

1932 Build house, Casa Genotta, at Sea Island, Georgia.

1933 *Ah, Wilderness!* is produced.

1934 *Days Without End* is produced.

1935 Begins his cycle of plays that examine American life, which includes *A Touch of the Poet, More Stately Mansions,* and "The Calms of Capricorn."

1936 O'Neill is awarded the Nobel Prize for Literature.

1937 The O'Neills sell Casa Genotta and buy land in Danville, California, and move into Tao House.

1941 Completes *Long Day's Journey into Night* and *The Iceman Cometh* at Tao House.

1942 Completes *Hughie* and *A Touch of the Poet.*

1943 Completes *A Moon for the Misbegotten.* Oona O'Neill marries Charlie Chaplin.

1944 The O'Neills sell Tao House and move to a hotel in San Francisco.

1945 The O'Neills return to live in New York City.

1946 *The Iceman Cometh* is produced.

1948 The O'Neills move to Massachusetts and buy a cottage on Marblehead Neck overlooking the ocean.

1950 Eugene O'Neill Jr. commits suicide.

1951 The O'Neills move to the Shelton Hotel in Boston.

1953 Eugene O'Neill dies 27 November. He is buried in Forest Hills Cemetery in Boston.

1956 *Long Day's Journey into Night* produced. The play is awarded the Pulitzer Prize.

1958 *Touch of the Poet* produced.

1964 *Hughie* produced.

Bibliography

Albion, Robert G., William A. Baker, and Benjamin W. Labaree. *New England and the Sea*. Mystic, Connecticut: Mystic Seaport Museum, 1972.

Bisset, Sir James, with P.R. Stephensen. *Tramps and Ladies*. New York: Criterion Books, 1959.

Black, Stephen A. *Eugene O'Neill: Beyond Mourning and Tragedy*. New Haven and London: Yale University Press, 1999.

Bogard, Travis, and Jackson R. Bryer, eds. *Selected Letters of Eugene O'Neill*. New York: Limelight Editions, 1994.

Bonsor, N.R.P. *North Atlantic Seaway,* vol. 3. Jersey, Channel Islands: Brookside Publications, 1979.

Boswell, Peyton, Jr. *George Bellows*. New York: Crown Publishing, 1942.

Boulton, Agnes. *Part of a Long Story*. Garden City, New York: Doubleday and Company, 1958.

Bowen, Croswell, with Shane O'Neill. *The Curse of the Misbegotten*. New York: McGraw Hill Company, 1959.

Breese, Jessie Martin. "A Home on the Dunes." *Country Life* (November 1923).

Bunting, W.H. *Portrait of a Port: Boston 1852–1914*. Cambridge, Massachusetts: The Belknap Press of Harvard University Press, 1971.

Clark, Barrett H. *Eugene O'Neill the Man and His Plays*. New York: Dover Publications, 1947.

Clements, Rex. *A Gypsy of the Horn*. Boston: Houghton Mifflin Company, 1925.

Colby, Barnard L. *For Oil and Buggy Whips: Whaling Captains of New London County, Connecticut*. Mystic, Connecticut: Mystic Seaport Museum, 1992.

Comens, Leslie Eric. Forward to Eugene O'Neill, *Chris Christophersen*. New York: Random House, 1982.

Cook, John A. *Pursuing the Whale: A Quarter-Century of Whaling in the Arctic*. Cambridge, Massachusetts: Houghton Mifflin Company, 1926.

Coogan, Jim. *Sail Away Ladies*. East Dennis, Massachusetts: Harvest Home Books, 2003.

Dalton, J.W. *The Life Savers of Cape Cod*. 1902; reprint, Old Greenwich, Connecticut: The Chatham Press, 1967.

Decker, Robert Owen. *The Whaling City*. Chester, Connecticut: The Pequot Press, 1976.

Deutsch, Helen, and Stella Hanau. *The Provincetown, A Story of the Theatre*. New York: Russell and Russell, 1972.

Doezema, Marianne. "The Real New York" in *The Paintings of George Bellows*. New York: Harry N. Abrams, 1990.

Dos Passos, Katherine, and Edith Shay. *Down Cape Cod*. New York: Robert M. McBride & Company, 1947.

Edwards, Agnes. *Cape Cod New and Old*. Boston and New York: Houghton Mifflin Company, 1918.

Egan, Leona Rust. *Provincetown as a Stage*. Orleans, Massachusetts: Parnassus Imprints, 1994.

Estrin, Mark W. *Conversations with Eugene O'Neill*. Jackson and London: University Press of Mississippi, 1990.

Flayhart, William Henry, III. *The American Line (1871–1902)*. New York and London: W.W. Norton & Company, 2000.

Floyd, Virginia, ed. *Eugene O'Neill at Work*. New York: Frederick Ungar Publishing Company, 1981.

Gelb, Arthur and Barbara. *O'Neill: Life With Monte Cristo*. New York: Applause Books, 2000.

_____. *O'Neill*. New York: Harper & Row, 1987.

Hamilton, Clayton. "American Playwrights of To-day." *The Mentor* (March 1923).

Haskell, Barbara. *The American Century: Art and Culture, 1900–1950*. New York: Whitney Museum of American Art in association with W.W. Norton & Company, 1999.

Hawthorne, Hildegarde. *Old Seaport Towns of New England*. New York: Dodd, Mead and Company, 1916.

Hibbard, Isaac Norris. *Sixteen Times Around Cape Horn*. Mystic, Connecticut: Mystic Seaport Museum, 1980.

Holland, F. Ross, Jr. *Great American Lighthouses*. Washington, D.C.: National Trust for Historic Preservation, 1989.

Howe, Octavius T., and Frederick C. Matthews. *American Clipper Ships 1833–1858*. 2 vols. New York: Dover Publications, 1986.

Hugill, Stan. *Sailortown*. London: Routledge & Kegan Paul, 1967.

_____. *Shanties of the Seven Seas*. 1984; reprint, Mystic, Connecticut: Mystic Seaport Museum, 1996.

"Imprisoned In Ice, Far From Home, At Christmas Time" and "Mrs. Cook's Christmas in the Icy North." *Boston Sunday Globe*, 24 December 1905.

Krutch, Joseph Wood. *The American Drama Since 1918*. New York: Random House, 1939.

Lloyd's Register of British and Foreign Shipping 1907/1908, 1909/1910 & 1910/1911. London: Lloyd's Register of British and Foreign Shipping, 1908, 1909, & 1910.

Lubbock, Basil. *The Last of the Windjammers*. 2 vols. Glasgow: Brown, Son & Ferguson, Ltd., 1953–54.

Macgowan, Kenneth and William Melnitz. *The Living Stage: A History of the World Theater*. New York: Prentice-Hall, Inc., 1955.

Maddocks, Melvin. *The Seafarers: The Great Liners*. Alexandria, Virginia: Time-Life Books, 1978.

Miller, William H., Jr. *The First Great Ocean Liners*. New York: Dover Publications, 1984.

Moffett, Ross. *Art in Narrow Streets*. Provincetown, Massachusetts: Cape Cod Pilgrim Memorial Association, 1989.

Morris, Paul C. *Schooners and Schooner Barges*. Orleans, Massachusetts: Lower Cape Publishing, 1984.

Norling, Lisa. *Captain Ahab Had a Wife: New England Women and the Whalefishery, 1720–1870*. Chapel Hill: University of North Carolina Press, 2000.

Oliver, Sandra L. *Saltwater Foodways*. Mystic, Connecticut: Mystic Seaport Museum, 1995.

O'Neill, Eugene. *The Calms of Capricorn: A Play Developed from O'Neill's Scenario by Donald Gallup With a Transcription of the Scenario*. New Haven and New York: Ticknor and Fields, 1982.

_____. *"Children of the Sea" and Three Other Unpublished Plays by Eugene O'Neill*. Jennifer McCabe Atkinson, ed. Washington, D.C.: NCR Microcard Editions, 1972.

_____. *Complete Plays, 1913–1920*. New York: The Library of America, 1988.

_____. *Complete Plays, 1920–1931*. New York: The Library of America, 1988.

_____. *Complete Plays, 1932–1943*. New York: The Library of America, 1988.

Quinn, William P. *Shipwrecks Around Cape Cod*. Farmington, Maine: Knowlton & McLeary, 1973.

Record of American and Foreign Shipping. New York: American Bureau of Shipping, 1910 and 1917.

Register of the United States Life-Saving Service. Washington, D.C.: Government Printing Office, 1 July 1914.

Register of the Officers, Vessels, and Stations of the United States Coast Guard. Washington, D.C.: Government Printing Office, 1915, 1916, 1917, and 1918.

Register of the Commissioned and Warrant Officers and Cadets, and Ships, and Stations of the United States Coast Guard. Washington, D.C.: Government Printing Office, 1920, 1921, and 1926.

Richter, Robert A. *Touring Eugene O'Neill's New London.* New London, Connecticut: Connecticut College, 2001.

Rogers, John G. *Origins of Sea Terms.* Mystic, Connecticut: Mystic Seaport Museum, 1985.

Ruckstuhl, Irma. *Old Provincetown in Early Photographs.* New York: Dover Publications, 1987.

Shay, Frank. *A Sailor's Treasury.* New York: W.W. Norton & Company, 1951.

Sheaffer, Louis. *O'Neill: Son and Artist.* New York: Paragon House, 1990.

_____. *O'Neill: Son and Playwright.* Boston: Little, Brown and Company, 1968.

_____. Papers. Shaeffer-O'Neill Collection, Charles E. Shain Library, Connecticut College, New London, Connecticut.

Smith, Nancy W. Paine. *The Provincetown Book.* Brockton, Massachusetts: Tolman Printing, 1922.

Thomas, Gordon W. *Fast and Able.* Gloucester, Massachusetts: William G. Brown, 1952.

Thompson, Courtney. *Massachusetts Lighthouses.* Mt. Desert, Maine: CatNap Publications, 1998.

Villiers, Alan. *The Way of a Ship.* New York: Charles Scribner's Sons, 1953.

Vorse, Mary Heaton, edited by Adele Heller with Jill O'Brien. *Time and the Town: A Provincetown Chronicle.* New Brunswick, New Jersey: Rutgers University Press, 1991.

Weibust, Knut. *Deep Sea Sailors: A Study in Maritime Ethnology,* 2nd ed. Stockholm: Kungl. Boktryckeriet P. A. Norstedt & Soner, 1976.

Whitmore, George. "The Washington Market." *Seaport Magazine* (Spring/Summer 1984).

Wilmeth, Don B., and Christopher Bigsby, eds. *The Cambridge History of American Theater, Vol. 2: 1870–1945.* Cambridge: Cambridge University Press, 1999.

Wissmann, Rudolff Walter. *The Maritime Industry: Federal Regulation in Establishing Labor and Safety Standards.* New York: Cornell Maritime Press, 1942.

Wolter, Jürgen C. *The Dawning of American Drama: American Dramatic Criticism, 1746–1915.* Westport, Connecticut: Greenwood Press, 1993.

Zabel, Barbara. "The Realist Revolution in Art: The Ashcan School." Unpublished paper, 2000.

Index (Page numbers in **bold** indicate illustrations)

A

Abbey Players, 75–76
Able Bodied Seaman, 39, 72
Ah, Wilderness!, 34
ambergris, 114, 173
American Line, 66–67, 158–59, 186
"Amindra," 151, 152–53
"Anna Christie," 21, 128, 129, 177, 182–85
Annie C. Perry, 118
Arctic whaling, 17, 110–15, 162, 163, 173
Argo, 21
Arnold, Benedict, 12
Ashcan School of art, 108
Ashleigh, Charles, 55
Atkins, Captain David H., 100, 125, 167
Atlantic and Western Steamship Company, 16
Atlantic House (Provincetown,
    Massachusetts), **109**

B

Baker, George Pierce, 87, 89, 147, 158
baleen, 17
Barracas (Buenos Aires), 55–56
Basso, Hamilton, 57
Before Breakfast, 109
Bellows, George, 35, 108
Beluga, 113
Bermuda, **130,** 131
Betts Academy (Stamford, Connecticut), 30
Beyond the Horizon, 116, 125, 128, 166–69
"Big Swede," 53
Black, Stephen, 28, 31, 34, 50, 128, 142,
    149, 182
Blyth, Jimmy, 77
Bolles, Nancy, 15
Boulton, Agnes, 77, 116, 118–19, 122, 126,
    127, 129, 130, 176
Bound East for Cardiff, 86, 106–07, 135, 141,
    146–50, 199
Bowhead, 110, 112
Bradley Street (New London), 31, 81
Brook Farm (Ridgefield, Connecticut),
    128–29
Brown, George Elmer, 102
Bryant, Louise, 105–06, 107, 108

Buenos Aires, **52,** 168; cattle trade of, 56–57;
    sailortown in, 51–56
bumboats, 153
Burdick, Captain William H., 16
Burns, Addie, 31

C

C.D. Boss Company (New London), 16
C.E. Trumbull, 100
"Call, The," 82
"Calms of Capricorn, The," 133, 190,
    196–97, 199
Cape Cod, 91
Cape Cod Canal, 95
Cape Cod Light (Truro, Massachusetts), 101
Cape Cod School of Art, 102
Captains Courageous, 30, 95, 144
Carlin, Terry, 89, 105
Casa Genotta (Sea Island, Georgia), 133
Casino (Buenos Aires), 55
Charles Racine, **38,** 40, 41, **42, 44,** 56, 82; 138,
    139, 187, 197; fishing on board, 46–47;
    food on board, 45; in storms at sea, 48–49,
    168; passage to Buenos Aires, 47–50;
    quarters on board, 44; work on board, 45
Children of the Sea, 86, 106, 147–48
Chris Christophersen, 21, 126, 128, 141, 166,
    175–81
Christophersen, Osmund, 50, 54
Christopherson, Chris, 74–75, 86, 150, 175,
    178, 183, 184, 187
Civil War, 17
Clark, Barrett, 153
Clarke, Everett Ladd, 101
Clements, Rex, 48
clipper ships, 40, 190, 195–97
coal barges, 19–**21,** 117, 177–78
coal trade, 18
Condon, James C., "Jimmy the Priest," 65,
    79, 183
Cook, Jig, 146
Cook, Captain John A., 110, **111,** 112–15,
    160, 161, 162, 163, 170, 173
Cook, Viola, 110, **111,** 112–15, 160, 161
Cook, William, 124

Count of Monte Cristo, The, 25, 87, 159, 174
crimping of sailors, 53–54, 151–52
crossing–the–line ceremony, 22, 47

D
Dakota, 18
Dalton, J.W., 100
De La Salle Academy (New York), 30
DePolo, Harold, 109, 156
Diff'rent, 128
Dodge, Mabel, 118–19
dogwatch, 149–50
Downes, Olin, 57, 201
Driscoll, 71–72, 74, 79, 89, 135, 165, 183, 186, 189

E
Edwards, Agnes, 102
Emperor Jones, The, 128
Endeavor, 11

F
Fairfield County State Sanatorium (Shelton, Connecticut), 83
Fall River Line, 102, 116
Farnsworth, Jerry, 126
Finnegan, Michael, "Mickey Finn," 53
First Man, The, 128
Fisher, Samuel, 100
fishing, 18, 91–95; hazards of, 94–95
Flying Cloud, 190, 196–97
Fog, 95, 109, 143–45
foghorn, 29
Fort Trumbull (New London), 191
Fountain, The, 128
Francis, John, 105, 116, 118, 121, 122, 128, 131

G
Gabrielsen, 150
Ganey, Dr. Joe, 34–**35**
Gaylord Farm Sanatorium (Wallingford, Connecticut), 83–84, 137
Gelb, Arthur and Barbara, 86, 142, 151
Glaspell, Susan, 106, 107, 108, 135
"*Glencairn,*" 110
Glencairn plays, 61, 63, 146
Gold, 128, 172–74
Great General Strike, 71
Great God Brown, The, 27

H
Hairy Ape, The, 46, 61, 68, 70, 72, 79, 89, 128, 129, **136,** 141, 145, 160, 165, 186–89, **187**
Hamilton, Clayton, 86

Hanson, 150
Harvard–Yale boat race, 32–**33**
Hawai'ian Islands, 14, 15–16
Hawthorne, Charles W., 102
Hawthorne, Hazel, 126
Hawthorne, Hildegarde, 11, 13, 32–33, 102, 174
Hell Hole (New York), 116
Herschel Island, Alaska, 113–14
Hettman, Frederick, 55, 56, 57
Holladay, Louis, 34, 40, 89
Homecoming, The, 191, 194
Hopkins, Arthur, 182, 189
Houghton Library, Harvard University, 158
Hugill, Stan, 51
Hunted, The, 195

I
Iceman Cometh, The, 133, 165
Ikala, 58–**59,** 146, 153, 177; life on board, 60–61; O'Neill as passenger on board, 58–59, 62; sailors of, 60
Ile, 23, 114, 116, 141, 160–64
In the Zone, 56, 61, 110, 116, 118, 150, 155–57

J
Jenkins, Kathleen, 37, 38, **76**–77
Jibboom Club (New London), 15, 22–**23**
Jimmy the Priest's (New York), 63, **64,** 65, 74, 77, 79, 89, 165, 175

K
Kalonyme, Louis, 37
Kanakas, 16, 172–73
Keefe, Ed, **35**
Keeney, Annie, 161
Keeney, David, 160
Keeney, Captain Nat, 23
Kelley, Charles P., 100
Kemp, Harry, 123
Knapp, James, 141–43

L
Latimer, Frederick P., 81, 82
Lawrence, Sebastian, 15
Learmont, J.S., 49–50
Lewisohn, Sam, 118–19
Liverpool Irishmen, 72
Long Day's Journey into Night, 25, 29, 31, 47, 83, 133, 161, 164, 167–68, 183, 201
Long Voyage Home, The, 54, 61, 110, 116, 150–53, 166
lumber trade, 42–43
"Lunger," 142

Lusitania, 156
Lyman, Dr. David R., 83–84

M

McGinley, Art, 164
McGinley, John, 25
McGinley, Tom, 34, **35**
Maggie Ellen, **81**
Marblehead, Massachusetts, 133, **134,** 135
Margarett, 12, 13,
"Mary Allen," 81, 171
"Mary Ellen," 81
Mayo, Frank A., 100, 125, 167
Men of the Docks, **108**
Mencken, H.L., 146
Merrill, Charles A., 76
Minnesota, 18
Moffett, Ross, 116
Monte Cristo Cottage (New London), 27, 81, 86, 135
Monterey, Carlotta, 77, **132,** 133, **136, 187,** 190
Moon of the Caribbees, The, 46, 110, 153–54, **155**
Moore, Tommy, 53
More Stately Mansions, 133
Morgan, Captain Ebenezer, 14, 15
Mourning Becomes Electra, 57, 133, 190–95
Mullett, Mary B., 65, 79

N

Navarch, 111
New Bedford, Massachusetts, 14
New London, 11–35, 81, 84–86, 174
New London Lighthouse, **10,** 29
New London Ship and Engine Company, 18
New London Telegraph, 81
New York, sailortown in, 63–66
New York, 66, **67**–68, **69;** crew of, 68; passengers on board, 68; stokers of, 69–70; transatlantic passage of, 70–71
Nichols, Dudley, 61
Nobel Prize for Literature, 133

O

O'Neill, Ella, 25, **26,** 28, 81, 84, 86, 129, 161, 172, 201
O'Neill, Eugene, **24, 29, 80, 85, 88, 106, 125, 127, 129, 130, 132, 134, 200;** and alcohol, 57, 64, 79, 103, 116, 131; and boating, 31, **80,** 84, 126, **130, 198;** and swimming, 31, 118, 124–25, 126; as Able Bodied Seaman, 72–73; aspects of in plays, 141, 159, 167, 182–83, 197; attempts suicide, 77; boards

with Rippin family, 84; childhood in New London, 27, 30–31; death of, 135; divorce of, 76–77, 81, 132; hospitalized for tuberculosis, 83–84; marriage of, 37, 116, 132; stops writing, 135; works read, 30, 34
O'Neill, Eugene Jr., 37, **76,** 128, 129, 132
O'Neill, James, 25, **26,** 27, **29,** 38, 63, 81, 84, 87, 105, 121, 128, 160, 161
O'Neill, James Jr., "Jamie," 27, **29,** 31, 84, 128, 129, 167
O'Neill, Oona, **130,** 131
O'Neill, Shane, **127,** 128, **130**
Ocean Beach (New London), 31, **32**
Olson, 150–53, 175
Ordinary Seaman, 39, 72

P

pamperos, 49–50
Paseo Colon (Buenos Aires), 57
Paul Jones, 19
Peaked Hill Bars Coast Guard Station, 122, **123**
Peaked Hill Bars Life–Saving Station, 98, **99,** 100, 118, **120,** 121–26, 131, 132, 169, **200;** legends of, 124
Pennistone, 118
Pequot Casino (New London), 26–27, **28**
Pequot Colony (New London), 26
Pequot House (New London), 26, 27
Personal Equation, The, 87, 89, 141, 158–60
Perth Amboy, 117
Philadelphia, 68, 69, **71;** O'Neill on board, 72
Pioneer, 14
Playwright's Theater (New York), 108
Port of Spain, Trinidad, 61–62
Princeton University, 33–34
Prostitution, 31
Provincetown, Massachusetts, 89, **90, 92, 93, 96–97, 100–01;** as art colony, 102; as fishing port, 91–95; as summer colony, 131; as whaling port, 92
Provincetown Players, 107–09, 116, 147, 150, 160, 169, 170, 186
Pulitzer Prize, 128, 129, 166, 182

R

Race Rock Lighthouse, 82–83
Reed, John, 105–**06,** 107, 108
Revolutionary War, 12
Rice, Captain John, 15
Rio de la Plata, 49, 51
Rippin, Emily, 84, 85
Rippin, Jessica, 84, 85
Rippin family, 84–85, 142

Rockmore, Robert, 56
Rogers Boat Shop (New London), 16
Rope, The, 116, 169–70
Rose Dorothea, 118
Ross, John 15

S

Sailing Alone Around the World, 164
Sailor's Opera, 54–55
sailors vs. stokers, 184–85, 186–88
St. Aloysius School (Bronx, New York), 30
St. Louis, 78, 165
"*St. Paul,*" 165
schooner barges, 20, 75, **99,** 178, 182
Scott, Maibelle, 82, 85, 167
Scott, Thomas Albertson, 82–83, 167
sea chanteys, 22–23, 45–46, 154, 165, 192–95
Second Engineer, The, 87
Second Officer, 141, 180
Second Story Club (New London), 34–35
Shanghai Brown, 151, 197
shanghaiing of sailors, 53–54, 151
Sheaffer, Louis, 30, 40, 53, 57, 59, 77, 105, 109, 138, 171, 186, 189
Sherwin, Louis, 156
shipbuilding, 18
Skinner, Richard Dana, 146
Sloan, John, 108
Slocum, Joshua, 164
Smith, Francis Hopkinson, 83
"Smitty," 56, 165
Sniper, The, 109
Southampton, England, 66–67, 71
Sparks, Ethel, 115
Stanhope, Frederick, 181
Strange Interlude, 77
Straw, The, 126

T

T. A. Scott Company, 83
Tao House (Danville, California), 133
Taylor, Elisha, 100, 125
Thames River (New London), 11, **20–21, 24,** 32, **33, 87**
Thames Tow Boat Company, **19**
Thirst, 107, 139–41
Thirst and Other One Act Plays, 86
Timandra, **36,** 56, 149, 152
Time and the Town, 91
Titanic, 138, 140, 142
"Tomorrow," 56, 110, 164–66
Touch of the Poet, A, 133
Tyler, George C., 63, 75, 128, 181, 182
Tyrone, James, 25, 161

Tyrone, Jamie, 31
Tyrone, Mary, 29, 161, 183

U

U. S Coast Guard, 18, 95
U.S. Life–Saving Service, 18, 95, 98–101; duties of, 98; hazards of duty, 100; methods of rescue, 98, **123**; stations of, 98, **99**
U.S. Lighthouse Service, 95, 101
U.S. Navy, 18, 101, **117**
U.S. Revenue Cutter Service, 18, 95
U–boats, 110, 117, 155

V

Viola, 114
Vorse, Mary Heaton, 91, 94, 95, 102, **103,** 106–07, 108, 110, 112, 115, 117, 124, 126, 131

W

Waage, Captain Gustav, 40–41, **42**
Waage, Severin, 51–53
Warnings, 141–43
Warren, James C., 76–77
Washington Market (New York), 66
Washington Square Players, 116, 150, 155
Webster, E. Ambrose, 102
Welch, Marion, 30
West Indies trade, 12
West Point Pleasant, New Jersey, 119
whale oil, 17
Whale Oil Row (New London), 191
whaling, 12–17, 162
Wharf Theater (Provincetown), **104,** 107
Where the Cross Is Made, 81, 116, 119, 128, 170–72
Williams, John D., 166
Winther, Sophus, 201
women aboard ship, 15, 110–15, 162
Woollcott, Alexander, 166
World War I, 117, 155

Y

Young, Isaiah, 100

Z

Zion, New Jersey, 35